Possible Autism

Susan Louise Peterson

Copyright 2015 by Susan Louise Peterson

Possible Autism

Susan Louise Peterson

CONTENTS

Preface vii

Prologue ix

Acknowledgements xi

Introduction 1

Chapter 1: Possible Autism Attributes 3

Chapter 2: Possible Autism Features 23

Chapter 3: Possible Autism Connections 43

Chapter 4: Possible Autism Aspects 63

Chapter 5: Possible Autism Indicators 83

Recommended Reading for Autism 103

Afterword 113

PREFACE

Having written two previous books on autism (***Questionable Autism*** and ***Is My Child Autistic or Delayed?***) I felt there was a need to explore some other possibilities of autism. When big increases in autism are reported by various agencies and organizations it makes me think about the possibilities that a child may have autism or possibly another delay, disorder or condition. I have always ruled on the side of 'caution' when anything related to children involves a hard and fast rule or decision. Children develop at different times and some are 'slower' to bloom, while other children take off at an earlier age. If we quickly determine a child's eligibility or even suggest that a child definitely has 'this or that' delay, disorder, syndrome or condition that child may prove us totally wrong in a few years when changes are made in his or her development and learning starts to come together for the child. The book ***Possible Autism*** emphasizes that we need to examine more possibilities related to autism and other types of conditions.

I once heard a developmental psychologist at a workshop mention that his clinic never made any determination on a child's condition or made a treatment recommendation until the staff had seen the child for several months. The reasoning behind this thinking was to take more time to get to know the child and have a greater understanding of the child's symptoms as well as environmental and family issues and how the child interacts in home and school settings. In the book, ***Possible Autism*** I look at a number of parent issues where parents are concerned about certain ways their children behave or react to various situations. I try to look at these parent issues from a school psychologist's point of view. As a school psychologist, I see that there are many 'other issues' that impact a child's life and how he or she is behaving or reacting to a situation. A child's behaviors or actions can resemble one condition or be part of a bigger more complicated picture that needs more observation and discussion before a school eligibility and planning decision is made for the child.

PROLOGUE

Working as a school psychologist for years I have heard a number of teachers and parents suggest that mistakes were made related to eligibility and placement of children in school special education programs. Many of their frustrations and concerns came from observations that the child acts differently than others with the same disorder or presents with different issues than the original school eligibility indicates in reports. Perhaps it was how professionals originally viewed the signs and symptoms of the child and then progress was made and the child responded well to interventions or no longer displays the symptoms first noticed by the team looking at the really young child. This is readily seen in young children who will not talk at all and then a few years later their vocabulary and language used to communicate greatly increases. Delays in children can be temporary or last for long periods of time so the possibility of a particular eligibility may be even more difficult to determine.

Possible Autism is meant to look at the likelihood that a child may have autism or possibly there could be an alternative disorder or delay that impacts or describes the child's condition. Possibilities can surround the particular attributes or characteristics of a child, but these possibilities can also be impacted by factors such as ineffective preschools programs, parents who lack parenting skills and strategies and the general community situation of the child. Sometimes a child's cues are misinterpreted by the professionals working with the child. A professional lacking experience with young children may misjudge a child's symptom as being autism or another disorder when it may actually be a delay in the areas of socialization or communication. When parents and professionals misinterpret information it can cause the child to be placed in an inappropriate classroom or a program that stifles the child rather than placing a child in a program where he or she can reach his or her full potential.

ACKNOWLEDGEMENTS

I cannot help but thank the countless education and clinic professionals who have taught me so much about autism and other conditions that impact children. Sometimes just a brief comment, a different angle in looking at a child and an encouraging word has helped clarify so many things about a child. These professional friendships are something I will always value as I reflect on my career as a school psychologist and educator.

I want to thank my wonderful husband and beautiful twin daughters for their ongoing support in my writing career. As my daughters are finishing high school and preparing for college, I hope they will continue to understand the importance of self expression through writing and the many avenues of whatever creative outlet they discover in life's path. My family is precious to me and continues to be a supportive part of my writing process.

INTRODUCTION

Parents will sometimes walk into an early childhood development clinic with three perspectives. One perspective is that the parent had no clue about autism-and hasn't really noticed any signs or characteristics of autism in the child. The second perspective is the parent who interprets everything the child does as autistic. For instance, if the child doesn't make eye contact or talk it must be autism and no other possibilities are even looked at when describing the child to the professionals. The third perspective is that of parents who are really confused by the different things professionals have told them. These parents may have been given some information that just does not jive with what they see in the child. Often these parents will start reading information on various websites and most of these parents are sincerely trying to make sense of the information on autism and developmental delays and how these things present in their own children.

The book, **Possible Autism** hopes to help parents, college students and professionals explore some common parent issues and concerns from a school psychologist's point of view. I think as an author and a school psychologist that I always like to note 'caution' before jumping to immediate conclusions about children. Sometimes I need to make an additional observation of the child or interview a parent or preschool to gain a better picture of how the child behaves at home or in a preschool setting. There are times I want to consider other possible delays or conditions with my multidisciplinary assessment team before the team considers autism as the educational eligibility. Team members are great to explore if other avenues should be considered in developing the child's educational plan.

Possible Autism is just the beginning point to consider matters that may be at play when a parent issue is brought up during the assessment process.

CHAPTER 1

POSSIBLE AUTISM ATTRIBUTES

Chapter one takes a look at possible autism attributes in children. I try to focus on some traits and characteristics that are sometimes 'clear cut,' but at other times are somewhat questionable in relationship to autism and other disorders. Even an attribute as simple as a smile can be misinterpreted by professionals who may or may not understand a child's 'social smile.' By the same token, the attribute of humor in the child can easily be interpreted in more than one way when the child is observed in the school or home setting. The eyes are another attribute that really opens up discussions related to autism and other delays. How the child uses his or her eyes to explore a room, make eye contact with others and stare at various objects are certainly topics for discussion. The topic of 'control' is looked at in relation to autism attributes in two ways. First, self control is examined with a look at how the child controls him or her self in relation to different situations. Second, control is looked at in connection with the child's 'intent' or understanding of a situation. The chapter continues to explore a variety of autism attributes related to change and flexibility and how children can have sporadic behavior in different situations and difficulties with transitions. There is a look at rote skills and how a child memorizes information versus how a child uses information in more useful and practical ways with other people. The chapter also examines preferred activities, sensory issues, tendency of being alone or withdrawn, as well as discussions related to empathy and atypicality.

Possible Social Smile

Parent Issue

My daughter smiles when she gets a new toy. Her developmental specialist thinks there are autism concerns, but I'm not sure about it.

A School Psychologist's Point of View

A smile can be interpreted in many ways. Smiling at a toy, may not always be a true indication that a child has what is considered a 'social smile.' Some children often smile at toys or objects, but not at the people who work with them. A smile may be observed as the child shows excitement or pleasure for a toy or specific activity. However, I would observe to see the child directs the smile toward others in a room. Did the child only smile at a doll during a game or was the smile observed when interacting with a person who initiates a game? Was the smile used as a social greeting upon arriving or leaving a room with other people. Professionals usually observe the child in social settings to see if a smile was directed more to objects or if it was used as an attempt to have some type of social interaction with other people. There can be periods of inconsistency with a smile. A child may only briefly smile at a parent of a familiar person and not smile at all to an unfamiliar person. As well, situations vary and a child may smile in a familiar, relaxing situation and not in an unfamiliar or stress type of situation. Professionals are often observing a child in various play activities to see if this social smile is directed toward other children or adults or to see if it is limited to an object or toy. The social smile can be an attempt to communicate with others or a sign of possible autism if it is directed more at objects than people.

Possible Humor

Parent Issue

My daughter does not respond to funny things. I wonder if this could be autism or some kind of developmental delay?

A School Psychologist's Point of View

Humor is an interesting subject to observe in children. Their responses to humor can sometimes be varied for many reasons. Some children don't respond to humorous jokes because they don't hear the punch line clearly or they have auditory processing issues where they only hear bits and pieces of a joke. There are some children with very introverted personalities so they don't want or need a strong 'jovial' or 'happy' environment with lots of jokes. As, well there are children with low intellectual disabilities that may not really understand the difference between a joke and an actual statement of truth. Autism concerns are sometimes noted in relation to humor. For example, a child unaware of his social environment may not even notice that classmates are telling jokes or acting in a silly way. The child's responses to social cues may also be noted in relation to humor. A parent may observe if a child stares off blankly during a funny activity or if the child has a delayed response to a joke. The teacher may be observing if the child can understand both the verbal part of the joke and nonverbal elements of the person telling the joke. Did the child understand things like eye contact, a funny hand gesture or unusual look or even the posture of a person in relation to the words in the joke or funny saying by another person? Professionals are watching to see if the child is self-absorbed or starts to notice, respond or react in some way to a humorous or joke-type situation. This is not always an easy task and takes some time to observe the child in humorous situations.

Possible Eye Exploration

Parent Issue

My son seems to look at objects so I think he is studying the features of the object or possibly how the object works. I think he is just curious and that he does not have autism.

A School Psychologist's Point of View

Eye movements may or may not be associated with autism. There can be autism concerns when children stare at objects for various lengths of time. The staring can be associated with the movement of an object, with a particular color or feature of an object or even the direction or position of an object or toy. There are even times a child may stare and it is not at any item or toy. This is difficult for parents to understand because there seems to be no purpose in why the child stares into space. The social intent of the eyes exploring or not exploring when someone else points to something is sometimes discussed as a concern in autism and gaining the child's attention. The range in which a child looks at objects is noted in their exploration of an item. There are even times when a child looks at objects from a very close range. He or she may put toys close to the eyes or move close to the television by actually putting the eyes and face right up to the television screen. There is always the question of curiosity and whether the child just wants to know how the television works and uses his or her eyes to explore this object. There is also a child who looks away from a person or activity, turning his or her head away and then looking back at something from the corner of his or her eye. If children are curious, they may look at an object for a longer period of time to explore how the object works or operates. The eye exploration of the child can give us lots of information in how the visual surroundings are processed and observed by the child.

Possible Eye Contact

Parent Issue

I have seen my son make eye contact numerous times. I don't understand why people are saying he has autism when he makes eye contact with his toys.

A School Psychologist's Point of View

Eye contact is both an interesting and sometimes a difficult concept to understand. Professionals may be observing if the child makes 'sustained and continual' eye contact versus 'fleeting or very brief' eye contact. Professionals sometimes disagree about the eye contact of the child. One professional may see eye contact as fleeting and another professional sees a more sustained type of eye contact. Sometimes professionals need to observe the child for a longer period of time in order to get a better picture of the child's eye contact. These professionals are also observing if the child makes eye contact with people in social types of settings. Some professionals may be determining if the child has poor or limited eye contact or if the child makes eye contact on numerous occasions. There are situations where the child will make eye contact with a familiar person and totally ignore and turn his or her eyes away from an unfamiliar person. Some children warm up, not giving contact at first and then establishing eye contact after warming up to a situation. Eye contact can be generated by the child to gain attention, understand facial expression and can be used to start or stop an activity. Parents sometimes forget that eye contact can be used as a response to show interest in someone else or show an intent to communicate with another person's request. When eye contact is limited to toys or objects, the social component of eye contact is left out of the child's interaction with others. Eye contact can be powerful in responding to the interest of others as well as learning about social cues.

Possible Staring

Parent Issue

My child has staring off episodes where she looks at certain things for long periods of time and I don't understand what she is doing.

A School Psychologist's Point of View

The subject of staring blankly at objects or just staring away from objects has been discussed all over the board by many different fields. One issue with staring off is that of 'what is the purpose or point of looking at the object?' If a parent is trying to figure out why the child is looking off into the distance he or she may look to see if the child is showing an intent to find out something about an object or toy or if the child is randomly starring at an object or going from object to object with no purpose. There are also visual movement issues related to staring at objects. I have assessed many children for autism and noticed these children staring at water bottles on my desk. I have never been quite sure what the interest is in the water bottles. For instance, I didn't know if it was the movement of the water in the bottle or the colorful label on the water bottle that attracts these children to the water bottle. Another scenario is that the child may want a drink of water so he or she just stares at the water bottle because the child is unable to ask for a drink of water. At the same time, a person cannot rule out that staring off may be associated with a medical condition. For example, staring has often been found in relationship to possible epilepsy or a seizure disorder. On the other hand, staring off may be an attempt to avoid or turn away from making social interaction with another person. A child may stare for a short period of time or look at objects for longer more intense periods of time. Autism includes social and communication deficits so staring off could be used to avoid this type of interaction with others.

Possible Control

Parent Issue

My son doesn't speak when I ask him a question-he seems to control what he says and this makes it difficult to communicate with him.

A School Psychologist's Point of View

There are some children who can master and take control of situations by the way they communicate or behave around people. Some young children learn very quickly that they don't have to speak, but just pause long enough for mom or a big sister to hand them the toy. These children have basically controlled the situation without initiating a request or responding to a request. Sometimes a parent will think that a child has autism because he or she tantrums. However, sometimes professionals will notice lots of 'intent' related to a child's tantrum. The child may be observed to tantrum when a direct request is given, but is fine when he or she can do his or her own thing during free play. The tantrum can sometimes become the child's 'controlling device' to notice that others will give into his or her bad behavior if a tantrum is played out to even a simple request. There are some children with autism who tantrum to communicate and are totally unaware of the tantrum as a controlling mechanism for others. A child with autism may 'act out' with a tantrum because he or she doesn't understand the practical rules of communicating with others. This child may not understand 'give and take' situations with other children and adults. A child with autism characteristics may lack the communication skills to participate in a conversation and may just repeat words or phrases. This is somewhat different from an unrelenting child who controls his or her parents by asking 100 times for the same toy over and over until the parents break down and buy him or her the toy.

Possible Self Control

Parent Issue

My young daughter can handle some situations by herself, but at other times she needs help to get her through the day.

A School Psychologist's Point of View

In looking at young children, parents and teachers should be cautious in thinking a child has self control. Sometimes young children will appear to do things in a routine order and seem to have self control when he or she actually exhibits some uncertainty with safety situations or routine directions. A teacher might notice in one situation that a kindergarten age child appears to be able to find the school restroom (down the hall from the classroom) by him or herself. The child may actually go once by him or herself and actually makes it back to the classroom. However, on another occasion the teacher might assume the child could find the restroom and he or she actually wanders off campus or to another part of the school. Self control in children can be situational. A parent may notice that a child has good self control skills in recognizing 'stranger types of danger' and would avoid a stranger in a grocery store. In another situation, the child's self control skills may not be as strong and the child may follow a stranger down the street without thinking to try and play chase with a stranger. Children may behave in different ways around various teachers and adults in their lives. They may appear more playful, carefree and unconcerned about danger in some situations and in other situations they appear more adapted to the routines. There are times a child has more self control in a routine, structured school setting where limitations are emphasized. This child may have difficulty with self control in a home setting with no boundaries or structure. A person must not make too many assumptions about self control without observations in structured and unstructured settings.

Possible Intensity

Parent Issue

My daughter does the same thing over and over again-so should I be concerned about autism or something else?

A School Psychologist's Point of View

In observing children, professionals are exploring the intensity a child uses when playing with toys or observing objects. Some children have no interest in a particular toy and just play with toy after toy with 'no purposeful' play. This would be a child who takes all the toys off of the shelf, but has no focus on the actual toys or how to use the toys. On the other hand there are children who are preoccupied or overly focused on a particular toy or item. This over intensity or being too focused on a toy may be a sign of possible autism. If a child stares blankly at a toy for longer periods of time, ritualistically plays with a toy in a certain way or repetitively builds a pattern with no flexibility to change then autism may be looked at in an assessment. Intensity may involve more than just being overly focused on a toy or object or the child's reaction to a change in the position of an object. Professionals may notice the child's intensity about order and how the child responds to a different order or pattern of the toys. The professional may look to see if the child adjusts to changes or a slight adjustment of the toy or adapts easily to the change or alteration. The child's intensity can range from being strong and unbending about some things and disinterested or easily accepting of a modification or change of things. A child could stare with intensity at household items or move his or her interest to a variety of people and objects in the home or preschool. The professionals must make observations to get a picture of the child's intensity about change or fixation with items to understand autism concerns.

Possible Flexibility

Parent Issue

My son is so rigid about everything that he is not flexible to change. He seems to want everything the same way all of the time.

A School Psychologist's Point of View

When looking at a child's flexibility there are several things to consider. Some children have difficulty being flexible to change because they have transition difficulties. Sometimes these children change easily in certain situations, but have difficulty making a change from a preferred activity or a favorite television show. There are parents who have shared that their children have sporadic behavior, meaning that they are fine in some situations and have a full blown tantrum on another day or at a different time. These children are more volatile with their coping skills and are all over the board with their responses to changes. Autism concerns can also be noted when related to flexibility and change. For instance, when a child has an insistence that everything needs to be the same way everyday there is an obvious inflexibility to change or a slight adjustment in a routine schedule or activity. The child may be lining up toys in a particular order as a calming technique, so when a change or distortion is made with the toys the child may have a melt down or tantrum. Lack of flexibility can also be seen when a child has a strong interest in a particular toy or subject area and the child has difficulty focusing on other interests. Lack of flexibility may be noticed in how a child responds in speech and language situations. Sometimes a child will be inflexible by only repeating a certain phrase for every situation. Inflexibility can be observed differently in children, but professionals are often looking at rigid, restricted and unbending interests as part of autism.

Possible Rote Skills

Parent Issue

My daughter knows her colors and numbers so well so she couldn't have autism because she is such a bright child.

A School Psychologist's Point of View

There are times when parents interpret a child's amazing ability to learn rote information as major progress in the child's development. Sometimes a parent relates a child's fantastic memory skills and ability to retain information as the total picture of progress. However, in looking at the whole picture of the child one must go a step further to see how the child uses the information that he or she has learned. One could question if the child can take the information and use it in a useful or practical way. A child who can use the information on colors of objects when sorting and building towers of various colors with a partner may be communicating information about colors in an appropriate learning setting. A child may never answer a question about the rote information he or she is learning, but may repeatedly sing the words of a color, number or alphabet song. Another child playing a counting game in a group activity may be showing other skills such as waiting his or her turn or learning to work with others on a team math project. It is great that a child has strong memory skills and the ability to learn information quickly, however the next move is to see how these rote skills can be transferred into more practical and interactive educational experiences. There are some children with autism characteristics that have great rote skills, but don't use then in any practical or useful way. The key is watching and observing the child at home and in preschool settings to see if this ability to learn rote skills and information is transferrable to other situations and interactions in the child's life.

Possible Preferred Activities

Parent Issue

My child only plays with toy horses and that is the only activity he shows preference to during the playtime at preschool.

A School Psychologist's Point of View

When a child shows a preference for a certain toy or activity several things can be occurring in the child's life. One possibility is simply that the child is curious and interested in the toy or object so he or she is at a learning point of exploring how an object works or understanding the characteristics of a toy animal or object. However, when a child has a preferred interest in an object or activity there can be some behavioral issues. The child may not want to play with other children and then tends to take the toy or object to a corner or play alone with the object away from other children in a preschool setting. The child may also start to fuss or tantrum if another child attempts to play with his or her toy. This child may lack the skills to share and take turns so the preferred activity can become a source of disagreement between young children in a day care or preschool program. Concerns of autism can be observed if the child is so possessive of a toy or object that he or she becomes isolated from other children with all of the focus on the toy or item. The child really lacks the interest in other children and the interest in the toy may even include a child using the toy in a repetitive process such as opening or closing an object numerous times, lining up toys or just showing an excessive interest in a toy or object. When a child has this excessive interest in an object the child can have difficulty with changing routines. It may not be noticed in the home setting where the child has free play, but in more structured settings there can be more resistance to a change from a preferred activity.

Possible Sensory Issues

Parent Issue

My child is so anxious that I think he has sensory issues related to autism or some other condition.

A School Psychologist's Point of View

There are times when parents confuse sensory issues with other behavioral issues like anxiety, hyperactivity or attention problems. At times a developmental specialist may make an assumption that if a child moves from toy to toy it could be because the child has sensory issues related to texture. I think professionals are looking to see if the sensory issues are obvious and over riding the behavioral issues. A professional may quickly notice a child 'mouthing toys' or sniffing toys before he or she plays with them. Taking off shoes or reacting to the fabric or tag in a shirt is usually obvious to most professionals. Sensory issues can be confusing if a parent learns a child will do a task for a certain type of food and then the parent offers the same food often to the child in a way that 'conditions' the child and gives others the impression that a child only eats certain foods. What happens at other times is that a child may move from task to task because he or she is hyperactive or has a very short attention span. A child may be anxious about attempting new tasks so it looks as if he or she is 'worried' or avoiding certain sensory experiences. Children may not touch an object because they are worried about getting in trouble from their parents. This avoidance may be from anxiety or nervousness about a toy or texture rather than a sensory issue. It is important to look at the whole picture of the child's behavior related to sensory types of issues as some sensitivity to objects may be justified in some situations and other sensory issues may need more exploration.

Possible Aloneness

Parent Issue

My daughter does not join in with other children, she just plays alone and this is a big concern for me.

A School Psychologist's Point of View

A child who plays alone may or may not have characteristics of autism. Some children have introverted personality traits where they are focused more on inward thoughts. These children may play alone at times and appear as being quiet. These children may shy away from large group experiences in preschools and go by themselves where they can observe other children participating in games and activities. There are times when a child is alone because he or she lacks the social skills to initiate play and turn taking with other children. If a child lacks communication skills he or she may not know how to ask for help or initiate conversation with other children so he or she tends to play alone even when other children are present. Young children presenting with autism characteristics may be so alone that they ignore social cues like a person coming into a classroom or knocking on the door. Autism characteristics may range from a child playing alone and not responding to any children around him or her to a child who refuses to interact with other children who are smiling, laughing or making eye contact with him or her. Children with autism may present at times as children spending time alone and not forming attachments or relationships with those children and adults around them. These lack of attachments in children are really noticed by professionals as well as parents observing the child. A child who prefers to be alone can sometimes present as a child with autism, but at other times appears as a child with delayed social and communication skills.

Possible Withdrawal

Parent Issue

My child is very withdrawn from other children so I know that he must have autism since he is so distant from his classmates.

A School Psychologist's Point of View

There are times when an autistic-like behavior such as withdrawing gets confused with autism. For example, a child may intentionally withdraw from a group situation or from an activity when the teacher gives a request or direction. Sometimes the child is withdrawing to actually gain control of a social situation. These types of withdrawal may also signify concerns with anxiety. A child may withdraw because he or she is afraid of making a mistake. A child may withdraw from a social situation because he or she is afraid of getting in trouble. I once remember someone telling me about a young girl who would not go the cafeteria because she had a disagreement with a cafeteria worker. It took months of the child working with a counselor and she finally was able to go to the cafeteria with the support of her older sister by her side. This was a behavioral issue with withdrawal because the child had anxiety about a stressful situation. In this case the child was aware of what causes the anxiety and withdrawal. If a child is withdrawn to the point of being unaware of his or her environment or immediate surrounding there can be autism concerns. A child who withdraws to the point of staring intensely at some things or totally looking away from people in other situations may have deficits in social interaction or communication with others. A child who withdraws can be a tricky case for professionals looking at both autism concerns and other delays. There can be many things at play as people observe withdrawal as an intentional action or an internal concern.

Possible Empathy

Parent Issue

My daughter may have autism because she is so into herself that she doesn't show empathy for other children.

A School Psychologist's Point of View

A big part of socialization and communication involves being able to show empathy to other people. Even a very young child can notice when another child or adult is hurt or injured. The child may reach over and gently pat another child who is crying to show empathy or concern. This shows that child has an understanding of hurt or pain in another person. It shows that a child can 'reach out' with feelings toward another person. Sometimes child with autism have trouble showing empathy because it involves showing feelings outside of 'him or her' self. Empathy may be harder for kids who have difficulty making friends and being aware of other's feelings. Empathy seems to require that the child has some understanding of the social problems or concerns of others. Often a child will see and hear another child 'crying' from pain or from being hurt in an accident. However, children can have individual issues that impact their ability to show empathy. A child dealing with a traumatic event or neglect may be dealing with so many issues that he or she avoids reaching out with empathy toward others. Another child may just simply repeat words to express empathy without really knowing what to express with words. Immaturity could be an issue for the lack of empathy a child shows toward others. If a child is very young and totally eccentric and focused on his or herself, he or she may be so overwhelmed with the idea of 'self' so the awareness of others is not addressed or even considered as they child goes through this immature stage.

Possible Atypicality

Parent Issue

My child only eats certain types of food and is a very picky eater so I think he is atypical or possibly has autism.

A School Psychologist's Point of View

Some children are just a little 'atypical' or different, but seem to function pretty well overall. There are other children where 'atypical' types of behavior have a greater impact on how a child functions day to day. Some agencies seem to take more time to see how a child functions before a diagnosis or eligibility for services is determined. This is important because it gives professionals more time to see if a child's 'atypical' behaviors are persistent or just a passing, temporary behavior. Other professionals want to get to know the child to determine if the atypical behavior is caused by something. A young child may be irritated by a tag rubbing his neck in a particular shirt, but not really react to the tag or textures of other shirts. In this case the child is not showing a sensory reaction to all shirts, but rather a reaction to something uncomfortable in one shirt. A professional could also notice a child bumping into objects, but after a certain time notice the child is just making careless mistakes, not following directions, is inattentive to objects around him or her or just has some vision issues. There is a plus side to taking a little more time to observe these 'atypical' types of behaviors before an immediate assumption is made to suspect autism or another type of disorder as each child's situation is unique and personal. Professionals want to observe these 'atypical' behaviors in relation to the child's responses in certain types of environments and how the child reacts in various situations with people and new surroundings.

Questions to Consider

How can professionals more effectively understand attributes such as a smile, eye contact and humor as it relates to autism and other disorders?

What are some ways professionals could discuss 'rote skills' with parents and explain the importance of a child using these skills in a practical and useful way?

What are some strategies parents could use to help a child who withdraws from groups of child and often prefers to be alone?

Can you name some professionals who could help child deal with 'sensory issues?'

What types of support groups are available in your community to help children develop social skills and learn about 'empathy' toward others?

Additional Autism Exploration Topics

Facial Expression and Autism

Variation in Speech and Language Related to Autism

Autism and Depression

Motor Movements and Autism

Autism and the Ego-Centric Child

Eye Contact in Social Interaction

Understanding Blank Stares

Rote Skill Development and Autism

Autism and Non-Preferred Activities

Autism Withdrawal Issues

CHAPTER 2

POSSIBLE AUTISM FEATURES

There are many features of autism that are not recognized by parents. As well, there are many features of autism in the second chapter that can be explored for other possibilities than autism. In looking at these features chapter two begins with exploring parent expectations that a child has no issues or concerns related to autism. The chapter continues with a look at a variety of topics related to children doing things the same way, showing unusual or repetitive habits, being fascinated with certain toys and even being obsessive about their action or the way things are done with toys. The child who is excessive about the attention to small details or is oversensitive and picky about sensory related issues is also discussed in the chapter. As well, when looking at the features of autism one cannot forget how possible giftedness can be confused with autism features. Parent concerns and matters are discussed related to a child's possible communication delays, tantrums, sleep habits and time issues related to family events. Autism features are continued in chapter two when there is a discussion about how people react differently around various people and in different settings. There are also features discussed that are related to danger and a child's sense of boundaries in his or her surroundings. The chapter ends with a look at how a child's actions are observed and interpreted by parents and professionals. It is hoped this chapter provides useful information for helping to understand a variety of autism features.

Possible Expectations

Parent Issue

My son has no behavior or speech issues so I don't think he has autism. I don't know why the school keepings suggesting autism to me.

A School Psychologist's Point of View

There are times when parent or child expectations distort the child's real issues or concerns. A parent may say 'my child has no behavior issues,' but observations at an early childhood clinic noted numerous tantrums, refusal behaviors, aggressive hitting and biting. Sometimes parents get used to a child whining or crying continuously so they don't see it as a behavior concern when a professional may point out there are major behaviors that need to be worked on in an early childhood setting. In the same way, a parent may point out concerns with the child's intellectual abilities because a child is not picking up information as fast as his or her siblings did. At times the parents may have too high of expectations that the child should be performing at an advanced level. The other end of the continual is the parent who doesn't think the child knows anything. However, an educational evaluation may reveal the child's cognitive abilities are in the in average range. In relation to autism, the parent's expectations for the child are also confused by the child knowing information versus the child using information. Some parents have high expectations for the child to know 'a lot' of things like colors, letters, numbers or shapes, but beyond that their expectations go adrift. Professionals may be looking more in depth to see how the child uses information in a practical way. They want to see if the child can 'apply' learning to different situations that are not memorized or rote in nature. There is an interest to see if the child can transfer learning to different situations or respond when asked a question in a different way.

Possible Sameness

Parent Issue

My child likes to do everything the same way. He is very particular about putting toys in the same order each time he plays with them.

A School Psychologist's Point of View

In looking at the concept of sameness several things could be considered. A child with higher cognitive abilities may enjoy putting objects that are the same in groups with some organized thought. It is not uncommon for children to collect and put dolls or toy cars together in groups as they play. Teachers may ask young children to put all the trucks or cars in groups so the children are looking at items with the same features. A child who is very curious or interested in a topic may focus more in learning about dogs or dinosaurs than other topics. The concern comes when the child may become overly reactive when the order of the objects changes or if something different is put into a similar group or objects. For example, a toy cow joining into a group of toy horses could cause the child to become upset or have a tantrum. When looking at autism, young children are often observed to see if they are repetitively doing various things as they are playing or trying to interact with other children. When changes are happening in an early childhood preschool, teachers are looking to see if the child is adaptable to change or if the child has issues related to the sameness of objects by being ritualistic or unwilling to change the order or grouping of objects. There is a fine line between the child making connections and learning from the sameness of objects as opposed to putting the same items together with no real connections of practical applications for learning and communicating about the objects.

The understanding of children's concept of sameness is very revealing about their personality.

Possible Habits

Parent Issue

My son may have autism because he watches the characters on one television program many times.

A School Psychologist's Point of View

There are times when a child develops certain habits in his or her environment that may mimic the symptoms of autism. For instance, I think of the old friend called the 'television set.' Some very young children are in environments where their parents allow a habit to watch long hours of television and to watch shows repetitively. Therefore, when parent is asked if a child does something repetitively such as watching a television program over and over again there may be a suspicion as to whether a child has autism or whether the child and family have a habit of watching the television programs many times. A child who has a habit of tantruming often to get his or her way may have actually learned that he or she gets attention or gets his or way by the habit of tantruming. Habits can come in many forms. A child may present the same task with a varying habit or possible explanation. A child may appear to be messy in the play area to one person as he or she fails to pick up the toys. However, on parent interview it is revealed that no demands are placed on the child and he or she doesn't have to pick up toys in the home setting. A child with a poor habit of picking up toys should not be confused with a child who has autism and dumps out toys on the floor with no sense of purpose in a play activity. In the same way some children have varying habits for different people and won't pick up toys for certain people, but will follow clean-up directions for another person. This habit is different from a child who is rigid and restricted to only pick up toys with a certain type of clean up song or poem. Habits are a big part of the environment and should not be confused with restricted patterns of interests.

Possible Fascination

Parent Issue

My son is fascinated by cars. He likes all colors, styles and shapes of cars. Does he have autism because of this fascination?

A School Psychologist's Point of View

There are several ways to look at a child's interest or fascination with certain toys or objects. Sometimes it is just typical to like some things and lots of children enjoy certain things like cars, dolls and even dinosaurs. There are also children with high levels of cognitive abilities who are very curious about parts of toys and how toys work. For example, a gifted child may overly study a toy car by looking at the car wheels and parts to try and understand what makes the car move. Interest in certain objects or toys can be purposeful and productive. However, when a child is totally preoccupied by a toy there could be signs of autism as the child has very restrictive interests in one particular toy. The child may be overly interested in toy cars and then starts lining them up with a strong focus on the cars. If someone comes along and moves a car or mom accidentally walks into a line of cars disrupting the carefully placed cars there can be an overall tantrum. This happens because the child is very adamant and inflexible to change the order of the toys. This relentlessness attention for the toy cars comes across as an overly persistent and restrictive type of interest, rather than a child who just curious or enjoys playing with toy cars. A child's fascination with toys and objects can be observed as a learning type of distinction versus that of a child who is overly focused on objects without an application of the toy or object to the real world. These applications to real world and practical situations are helpful in understanding if a child has delays or possible autism.

Possible Obsessive Actions

Parent Issue

My son is obsessive if anyone changes anything about the order of his play toys and sometimes he will tantrum even if there is only a small change.

A School Psychologist's Point of View

When a child is very obsessive or overly focused on certain objects or toys there is often an immediate suspicion of autism. However, some children are obsessive about toys or objects for a variety of reasons. The child's situation could be one where a day care center or home has a limited number of toys. As a result, a child may be obsessive about keeping a certain type of toy in his or her possession and be unwilling to share or let anyone touch the toy. It is also important to note that some children may almost seem obsessive about a toy when they are really curious about how a toy works or a playful action from a toy. A parent will sometimes interpret obsessive interest of a toy from a child who is gifted or has higher cognitive abilities. Autism concerns with obsessive actions really focus on several things. Sometimes professionals will point out to parents that the child is excessive about the sameness of objects or toys. The child will only play obsessively with one type of toy or toys that are all the same. There are also issues in how the child plays with the obsessive toy. Does the child play with the toys appropriately or spend time lining up toys, taking apart or spinning toys or simply staring at toys obsessively. On occasion, a child will talk about the toy obsessively or say the word 'dinosaur' over and over. It is important to note that in general some children are slightly obsessive about their favorite toy or a toy they really enjoy. However, obsessive actions seem to be a big issue when it is excessive and the child is resistant to change, to being flexible or make any adaptations with a particular toy or object.

Possible Attention to Details

Parent Issue

My child has exceptional art abilities and notices very small details, but some people think he has autism.

A School Psychologist's Point of View

I think one of the most confusing things for parents is that there is a broad range of skills and ability levels in children who have an eligibility of autism or autism concerns. However, there are also an array of children with different talents in the general population. Perhaps when looking at autism several things should be noted. For instance, one could question if the child is overly reactive or displays extreme tantruming when a small detail is changed, moved or in a different order. A child can be particular about details, but not be ritualistic about the order of something. A child can certainly be protective of an art project that has taken hours to complete so the art project is not destroyed or damaged. A child protecting an art project from someone who might become destructive with it is simply preserving the art project from damage. However, a child that is fixated on small aspects or characteristics of an art project, forgetting the main focus or purpose of the project may show characteristics of autism. If a child stares at small objects for long periods of time or becomes fixated on a spinning art piece he or she may lose focus of other aspects in the environment and become overly involved in a ritual of repeating a task many times. When a child is overly concerned about small details there can be red flags about many areas such as anxiety (being worried, upset or fearful), autism (fixating on small details) or a variety of other conditions. There are many elements to look at when a child pays excessive attention to details.

Possible Oversensitivity

Parent Issue

My daughter seems to be annoyed by many sensory things and so picky about what she touches and what fabrics touch her skin.

A School Psychologist's Point of View

Children in general can be sensitive to some things in our environment. Some children can be very 'touchy' and want to touch and feel many textures, items or objects. A bit of this can be exploratory learning and schools often encourage this through hands on learning activities and discovery learning projects. There are children who have a greater awareness to sounds and noises than other children and some children are totally unaware of the sights and sounds around them. Sometimes the sensitivity to an item of clothing may be justified. If a child breaks out in a rash from wearing a dress or blouse with lace there may be a medical concern. The child may have a skin allergy to lace and the oversensitivity to the fabric may be justified as he or she turns red and does not prefer to wear the item of clothing to school. Autism concerns often come about when a child is observed to be over or under sensitive to various things in the environment. A child covering his or her ears, flicking his or her eyelids or flushing the toilet over and over starts to trigger red flags to parents. When a child shows this somewhat 'constant' sensitivity to objects and items parents can start observing and documenting these unusual types of actions to share with professionals conducting early childhood assessments. Parents will want to see if the child has a type of sensory disorder or if the sensitivity of objects is also related to significant delays in communication and social skills that could be related to autism. Some children also have developmental delays and may need support from an occupational therapist to learn sensory strategies to deal with a variety of sensory issues.

Possible Closeness

Parent Issue

The twin sisters are hugging each other, but at times they seem like they are bumping heads so I don't know if it is affection or a behavior problem.

A School Psychologist's Point of View

Observation is important in distinguishing whether closeness between children resembles affections, a behavior issue or even a sensory issue. I once heard a parent comment that she could not distinguish whether a set of twins were hugging each other or bumping each other's face. Sometimes it seems like kindness and affection at first and then turns into head banging each other or even biting each other. The affection may turn into a behavior issue or a contest of will power or taking over the other child. On the other hand, this closeness may also resemble a sensory issue of just rubbing cheeks or rubbing a hand over the other child's face in a repetitive manner. There can also be reactions between the children that start out as close and turn into strong contentions. Children can make eye contact briefly and then have a tantrum if someone else gets in their space or too near the toy the child is playing with in a center area. A child may have an unusual sensory response if another child stands very close and may have a scented spray in his or her hair. Children playing in a center who touch each other can exhibit reactions to even a slight touch, pain from movement or even a tactile type of resistance to a pat on the shoulder from a teacher trying to praise the child. A child with autism may have unusual sensory experiences that relate to both the closeness of people and the closeness of certain objects. The child may attempt to taste, smell or feel various textures, objects or toys in a play center or home environment.

Possible Giftedness

Parent Issue

My child is very smart (possibly gifted) and he is more interested in how toys work than playing with the toys.

A School Psychologist's Point of View

I knew at some point the topic or giftedness and autism would come up. Young children with very high cognitive abilities and preschool readiness skills often will present with some autistic like characteristics. Gifted children don't always fit into perfect learning styles and children who are gifted may seem a little atypical to some people. For example, a child who is curious about a toy may avoid eye contact and playing with other children to show an extreme interest in how the toy works. In this case the child is not avoiding eye contact and social interaction to withdraw from others, but exploring with intensity the aspects of the toy. This is showing the child is choosing not to make eye contact by choosing to be involved in the intense investigation of the toy. A person could easily mistake this intentional avoidance of eye contact and social interaction as autism when it is actually an interesting perspective of a gifted child and his or her own curiosity about the world. I have noticed this at times when assessing children with block building activities. For instance, some children with autism concerns will push blocks away or line up blocks instead of stacking the blocks on request. A very gifted child will sometimes not only stack the blocks, but replicate block designs from both a demonstration or a visual picture of blocks before the age of three years. This child may have unusual cognitive abilities that can resemble autism, but are actually more of a gifted feature where the child has a strong use of nonverbal cognitive abilities. As a school psychologist, I am always cautious when looking at autism eligibilities along with the gifted aspect in some children.

Possible Communication Delay

Parent Issue

My child has trouble communicating so I definitely feel that he has some kind of issues that might be related to autism.

A School Psychologist's Point of View

There are a large number of children who have communication delays. Some of these children have autism concerns and some do not. When a professional is looking at a child's communication skills he or she is looking at how the child uses words and understands words. Sometimes parents are confused because the child is saying so many words. The child with autism may know a lot of words, repeat many words and name many objects. However, many children with autism have major difficulties in expressing their views and ideas. These children struggle when asked an oral question or a question where they may have to explain the answer. The struggle with communication really comes into play in the preschool or day care environment when the child is challenged by many face to face encounters. These encounters may require social and communication responses that are difficult for the child. The child is expected not only to understand the request, but to respond to a give and take situation. This is why some professionals in the area of autism focus the importance of 'turn taking' as an essential skill that involves both communication and social interaction. Professionals can certainly observe young children to see if the child has a communication or socialization skill delay. This type of child presents different from a child with autism. A child delayed in communication may try to communication with others showing concern, using lots of gestures or trying to get attention, even though he or she lacks the vocabulary to express ideas. The professionals want to see attempts to communicate in a practical way.

Possible Tantrums

Parent Issue

My child tantrums constantly and some of the tantrums are so bad that I think it might be a sign of autism or something else.

A School Psychologist's Point of View

Sometimes a child displaying tantrums is mistaken for a child with autism. Yes, a child with autism may tantrum and many of these tantrums are related to disturbing the order of things or interfering with a repetitive routine that the child sees as having a calming effect. Children with developmental delays may also tantrum for many reasons. Children delayed in language may tantrum because they can't express what they are trying to say. Children with socialization delays may tantrum because they have fluctuating moods, aggressive behavior and are still learning transition skills. Sometimes children with low cognitive and intellectual disabilities tantrum because they are frustrated that they can't put together a puzzle or complete a block building project. As a result, a child may tantrum by throwing puzzle pieces that don't fit correctly into a puzzle or throw blocks because he or she doesn't understand the block building task. A child delayed in daily living and motor skills may also show tantrums. A child still learning toileting skills may show frustration with toileting routines. There are some children who have more severe tantrums when they are younger and can't express their needs. As some children grow older and talk more, the tantrums are sometimes reduced. Professionals will often notice communication and socialization delays in relationship to tantruming. If a child has motor delays a tantrum may occur as he or she struggles to run or jump. Tantrums can occur for many reasons and may or may not be associated with autism.

Possible Sleep Issues

Parent Issue

My daughter may have autism since her sleep patterns are all over the board and she gets out of bed all hours of the night.

A School Psychologist's Point of View

There are some children with legitimate sleep issues, while other children may have environmental issues that impact their daily living routines. If parents work split shifts or late nights the child may start to develop sleep patterns that shift to sleeping later or staying up later hours at night. This might not be an issue when a child is young and in a more carefree environment, but when a child starts to school and the bus arrives early in the morning the child's schedule will change. If a child goes to school without enough sleep, the child may present as fussy or with tantrum types of behavior as he or she tires throughout the day. Some parents misinterpret this fussy behavior as autism when it is actually related to routine and environmental sleep issues. There are children with autism who have sleep issues. Parents sometimes worry because some of these children are up in the middle of the night. Parents have reported incidents of children unlocking the doors and running in the streets during the early morning hours. Parents need to document and write down any unusual sleep occurrences of the child. Professionals working with young children can make suggestions and strategies that may improve the sleep and routine patterns for the child. If medical concerns are related to the sleep issues of the child then these will need to be addressed as well. Sleep can have a big influence of the educational success of a child and how he or she functions in the classroom. Sleep impacts a child's life in so many ways so it is important to understand if it is related to a specific disorder or if it is an environmental or routine issue.

Possible Time Issues

Parent Issue

My son has been withdrawn since his father died-so I think this has caused him to have autism and I am not sure what to do.

A School Psychologist's Point of View

There are times when children appear to be more withdrawn after a life changing event. Some children need more time than other children to process a major change in their lives. The change may turn out to be a mild alteration in the child's life style or it may be a major disruptive event. For example, a family situation of divorce (when a father was rarely around for the child) may not impact a child as much as another child who has lost a lot of contact with a close parent. The child may react to this disruption or change by tantrums, being unresponsive to social cues or just ignoring those around him or her. Therefore, a person may actually start to think a child has signs of autism. The reality is that the child just needs more time to adjust and process a major life changing event. These time issues can be big concerns for the child as some children will need more time to process a life changing event than other children. I have heard some mental health professionals say that they won't diagnose a mood or anxiety disorder until several months have passed to see if the symptoms are persistent. This allows time for the child to adjust more to a major life changing event. This important thing is that time allows a child to reflect on a big change even if the change seems small. A child moving to a new neighborhood in the same town may not seem important to parents, but it may be a big adjustment for a child leaving friends and going to a new school. Time to make a change and adjust to a new situation may be needed in different amounts for children with various personality types, age ranges and who have different perspectives about life.

Possible Differences

Parent Issue

My child may have autism because she acts differently around various people-sometimes she is shy and at other times she is talkative.

A School Psychologist's Point of View

There are times when children behave differently under various circumstances. A child can be well behaved at home or hard to redirect in a day care center environment. Some children talk and interact in some environments and become shy or close down in another surrounding. There are some children who make eye contact with certain people and avoid eye contact with others. Another example, of these differences can be seen in the communication area. A child may use words to name objects and repeat words, but not recognize the meaning of words. There are times when some children repeat words as meaningless expressions. The repetition is so obvious, but the connection to the meaning of words many not be obvious for children with autism concerns. Differences in a child's behavior may have to do with the comfort level around certain people in different social situations. In autism multi-team assessments, professionals will look at the frequency of certain behaviors. This helps see if a child withdraws frequently in social situations or if the child only withdraws in some situations. There are many variables in social situations. For instance, some children relate more to different genders. A child may respond more openly to a female professional than a male professional (or vice versa). On the other hand, a child with autism may turn away from everyone making a direct request and have limited social exchanges with most people. In looking at differences, parents and professionals will want to look at consistency of behaviors. The adults want to observe if the child acts differently in various situations or if the child is consistent across the board.

Possible Danger

Parent Issue

My son has no boundaries at all related to danger or taking risks, he is basically fearless and this concerns me.

A School Psychologist's Point of View

I often hear the topic of danger or risk taking behavior come up from parents discussing the child's behavior. As a school psychologist, I am often observing if the child has an awareness of risk taking behavior or if the child is unaware of the dangerous situations. I have noticed that some children run in the street who are fully aware that cars are coming, but have a risk notion of 'beating or out running' the car in the street. This is quite different from a child with autism who loves to run and is totally unaware of the dangers of running in the street. I think as a school psychologist I am looking to see if the child has a sense of understanding about boundaries and limits related to danger. A child playing with everything, pulling items off of the shelf and moving from toy to toy may be totally oblivious to dangerous situations. On the other hand, a child who knows a situation is dangerous may attempt to climb on a high shelf to gain attention or be defiant. A child with autism may climb on a shelf to reach a high lock and lack an understanding of the danger of the situation. Parents struggle to make sense of how the child understands danger, boundaries and limitations. Parents may make household adjustments to deal with the child's 'fearless' actions. There may be behavior strategies that can assist children who need help with defiant, rebellious and risk taking behaviors. Choices can be given to the child with safer activities that have boundaries and more specific limitations. As the child gets older the goal is usually to make more self directed safety decisions as consequences are discussed with the child.

Possible Actions

Parent Issue

My child was just waving his hand, but the school psychologist says it is hand flapping and possible autism.

A School Psychologist's Point of View

A child's actions are sometimes viewed differently by various professionals and parents. For instance, a parent might say the child flaps his or her hands, but a nurse may notice the child has an involuntary tremor. A speech therapist may notice the child flapping hands as a sign language symbol to mean 'all done.' There could be a difference in a medically related hand tremor and hand flapping as part of self stimulation and this would need to be discussed with medical professionals. Another action that is sometimes misinterpreted is head banging. There is the young child who has trouble communicating and may tantrum occasionally and bang his or her head with frustration. This may be different than a child who bangs his or her head repetitively as self stimulatory behavior. Parents should note any unusual behaviors or actions to professionals assessing or evaluating the child. Parents will be receiving information from the professionals observing the child to get their opinions regarding the child's actions. Professionals may note a child's action or response as a sign of autism and at other times they may see the action as a delay or even a typical behavior for the child. Sometimes a child's action or response may be more than one thing. For instance, some actions of children are integrated types of problems such as motor, visual or spatial integration issues and there may be a need to probe deeper into the child's actions. These children may need to work with different types of specialists to pinpoint their needs and gain more support in developing the child's educational program for a particular setting or school environment.

Questions to Consider

Can you think of some ways that could help a parent have realistic expectations for a child's education with autism concerns?

How can you explain to a parent that there are autism signs when the parent sees no issues or concerns?

What are some ways to redirect a child's attention from a preferred interest back to other preschool activities?

How can professionals distinguish giftedness from autism when assessing a child?

What are some disorders other than autism where children have tantrums?

Additional Autism Exploration Topics

Gifted Programs for Students with Autism

Redirection of Children's Interest in Different Topics

Conversational Skills for Students with Autism

Sleep Patterns of Children with Autism

Autism and School Safety Issues

Time Management for Children with Autism

Habit Changes and Autism

Changing Obsessive Behaviors

Parenting Strategies for Tantrums

Risk Taking Behavior and Prevention

CHAPTER 3

POSSIBLE AUTISM CONNECTIONS

Chapter three focuses on many connections that could be related to autism as well as other possible delays or disorders. For instance, parenting skills and family situations are discussed when looking at the picture of the child's connection to autism. Sometimes parents even request specialized services for autism concerns. There are some children who cannot or won't ask for assistance and need support in this area. These children may also have trouble generalizing their experiences to a variety of situations. A child may have limited experiences or lack experiences in a setting so he or she may appear to have delays or possible autism characteristics. There can also be autism connections to various places or settings where a child may behave or act differently. A child's participation could vary in a structured or unstructured setting. There are many connections related to social interaction This chapter examines relationship difficulties in children as well as how some children are engaged and disengaged in activities. There are children who have difficulty or lack interaction with others. They struggle to have shared attention and meaningful play experiences with other children. There are also elements of children having delayed responses that are considered as autism at first, but later on the child warms up and communication with other children and adults increases. The chapter ends with a look at a child's resistance to changing situations and there are certainly many factors that could influence a child's resistance to many types of changes.

Possible Parenting Skills

Parent Issue

My daughter just doesn't respond well to requests and I don't know if I should demand more out of her or could this be a sign of autism?

A School Psychologist's Point of View

A school psychologist is often trying to look at the whole picture of the child. Sometimes the picture of the child is looked at in context of the family and parenting skills. For instance, a child who is exhibiting pouting, whining behavior and easily gets frustrated may be imitating the poor coping skills of a parent with depression. This is also seen in younger children who have an older sibling, relative or parent with autism and these children may seem to show signs of autism, but are actually just mimicking some of the responses and behaviors around them. A child who is from a family with a mental health history may almost appear to have autism as the child fidgets or rocks back and forth in his or her seat or shakes his or her hands with excitement or fear. However, the same child may also be dealing with anxiety or hyperactivity. The child may also be role modeling the parent's behavior and reactions. A parent may describe the child as being unresponsive. However, a home visit may reveal that the parents were unresponsive to the child and they were slow to interact with the child, slow to give feedback and had a flat affect without a lot of facial expression. When a team interacts with the child they would understand why a child with an unresponsive parent would be unresponsive at times, but would also notice when the child is attempting to communicate even with poor role modeling or parenting skills. Looking at the child in relationship to the home environment would help professionals see the parenting skills in relationship to the parent's coping abilities, feedback and role modeling when evaluating for autism, developmental delays and other disorders or syndromes.

Possible Service Request

Parent Issue

My child gets a specialized autism treatment and I want the school district to continue and provide this treatment as a service because it really benefits him.

A School Psychologist's Point of View

There are autism therapies and specialized approaches that parents use when they have autism concerns for their children. The credibility of these diverse autism approaches is varied. Some of these autism approaches are supported with more evidence and research, while other approaches have very little research to support their effectiveness. While some autism treatments are well established, other approaches may appear as fads that come and go out of the limelight. Parents sometimes pay for these specialized autism treatments in different ways. Some parents pay for the treatments out of their own pockets, while others get insurance or government benefits to pay for the cost. There are times when parents start having high expectations that these specialized services will be provided for the young child once the child moves into the school setting. However, some parents are disappointed when school districts do not provide specialized autism treatments or services. Once in a while, a parent will request a school district to provide a specialized program that he or she likes to use for his or her child. Often school districts provide a reasonable and appropriate education for the child, but that does not include very specialized approaches to work with one child. An example, may be a parent requesting a specialized service or approach for one child that will need a teacher with a unique certification or specialized endorsement. However, if that teacher leaves the district or it the multidisciplinary team changes the placement for the child to spend half the day in a regular education class there would probably be no one 'qualified' to teach that one child with a specialized service.

Possible Assistance

Parent Issue

My son won't ask for help. He just plays and never seeks assistance or even asks the teacher to help him so I think he may have autism.

A School Psychologist's Point of View

A child's need to request or seek out assistance may be based on many things. A child may show signs of autism in a small office setting where he or she is pacing in the room and getting anxious about the small confined quarters. However, in a large preschool where the child has more space he or she may not pace back and forth at all and approach staff to get help with a toy. In one setting a child may not 'show' a toy, but in another setting the child may be willing to show something or ask for help. For some young children asking for assistance does not mean using perfect language and it might be just an utterance or sound with an attempt to communicate the need for assistance. Some children will try to get assistance with a gesture since they don't know the words or have the vocabulary to ask for help. A child may lack turn taking skills and have difficulty asking for assistance during a game or activity. A child throws the ball to another child and that child takes the ball and runs away with the ball. The child does not know how to seek assistance in the game. He or she doesn't know how to get the ball back for the game. The child may lack the skills to initiate assistance or help. Professionals are observing if the child shows the social awareness to ask for assistance by using gestures, words or some indication for help. The professionals are aware that some children are shy in some situations and would not ask for help, while they may be more open to seek assistance in other situations and with other people. The intent to seek assistance and help requires the child to reach out in some way with communication and socialization skills.

Possible Generalization

Parent Issue

My daughter understands some things very clearly, but doesn't generalize them to other situations and it is very frustrating.

A School Psychologist's Point of View

Generalization of information to different people and social environments is an important part of effective communication in social situations. A parent may not notice this at first in a young child who does well in a very structured routine. Some preschool elementary teachers are so organized and structured with each classroom routine or transition that a child with autism traits follows along well with repetitive rules, color coded centers and bells ringing to transition from place to place in the school. However, when these cues are removed or not followed the child 'falls apart' in a varied and unpredictable type of situation. When the repetitive routine is not followed the same way by a substitute teacher the child cannot accept a different order or adjusted routine in a daily schedule. In the same way, a child may not be able to generalize words to others. The child may not recognize a different person saying the same idea in a different way. A substitute teacher asks the children to line up and doesn't use the same line up song or words and the child doesn't know how to respond or generalize the words to a new 'line up' situation. The teacher may have taught the child to be a door greeter and say 'hello or welcome' to students as they enter the room, but the child does not generalize the 'hello or welcome' to parents, other teachers or guests who enter the room. Generalization is important in helping children with autism and delays become more observant in adjusting routines, observing others and becoming more aware and alert to changing social conditions that they will face on a daily basis.

Possible Experience

Parent Issue

I believe in keeping my son at home until he is six years old and now the school is saying he might have autism.

A School Psychologist's Point of View

I think it is important to note children's experience or lack of experience may influence how they are viewed in relationship to autism and delays. Of course, a young child who has received many home interventions and experiences with specialists since birth would be viewed in relation to how the interventions are working. A team assessing the child would be looking to see if the child made progress or if there is still a need for continued support in a school setting. Another issue that may pop up is the need to look at the child for a longer period of time in order to obtain data and make more observations of the child. For example, a child educated in the home setting may have had little or no social interaction with other children or some same age peers. This child, of course would present with socialization delays, but the reason for the delay in socialization has to do with having very limited social experiences with other children. There is a need to take time observing the child as he or she starts interacting with others to see if he or she responds to social requests or initiates play and social exchanges with other children. This documentation helps note if the child attempts to communicate with one or more children by initiating exchanges and developing friendships in the classroom. On the hand, this documentation can show autism characteristics in the child and provide a written, detailed log of behaviors and class observation notes. The team usually wants to see an indication of whether a child is self absorbed in his or her own world or if there is an attempt to reach out through communication and socialization efforts to function at school and in society.

Possible Behavior Changes

Parent Issue

My child just acts strange in some places and not in other places, this sure seems like autism to me and it really bothers me.

A School Psychologist's Point of View

Professionals are looking to see if children's behaviors present themselves across different conditions and settings. One professional may suggest sensory issues with a child's rapid movement from activity to activity. Another professional may see a very bright child who gets bored quickly and needs enriching activities to stay interested and focused in particular areas. When the child is in an engaging academic environment behaviors go down and when a child is not provided opportunities to learn he or she may become 'keyed up,' fidgety or be all over the place. Professionals may also be looking at different preschool conditions related to the child's reactions or responses. For example, a child who is disorganized, may learn strategies to follow directions in a preschool with more routines or organization. A child with attention and focusing issues may not respond well to a free play type of center where open choices are given and the child does not have time to focus on task completion. Children with autism vary in their skills and abilities so they may react to different teachers, classroom programs and schools in various ways. Good documentation of the child's reactions to different learning conditions will help provide valuable information to develop effective program placement. This documentation can also provide feedback on strategies that work and do not work well with the child in certain conditions. Children behave in different ways for a large number of reasons. A simple change in diet, sleep patterns, a move to a new place, a different teacher or classroom change can all influence a child's behavior on a given day.

Possible Settings

Parent Issue

My son behaves well at home, but is very different when he is outside of the home so I have some autism concerns.

A School Psychologist's Point of View

There are children who act differently in different settings. Some children are calm and talkative in the home, but become shy or un-talkative when they go to a social setting. Other children may present more consistently across settings. For instance, a child may be withdrawn in the home setting, also withdrawn in the preschool and continue to be withdrawn when at a grocery store. When a child has autism you will sometimes see the child has difficulty communicating and socializing in a variety of settings. It is the inconsistent types of behaviors that sometimes cause a parent to be suspicious that the child may not have autism. A child who withdraws the first ten minutes in a testing session and then warms up and makes eye contact would be displaying more appropriate communication and socialization than first recognized. A key to understanding how a child reacts and responds in a social setting is to view his or her pragmatic or practical communication and social skills when he or she is in a type of social situation. A child tapping on Dad's arm to be picked up is making a practical attempt to get his or her point across. When a young boy tugs on grandma's purse to get her attention and points to the shiny new truck on the shelf he is making an attempt to reach out. A parent may say 'she will do that for me at home,' but not complete a task for an unfamiliar person. Some children have consistent behavior in different settings, while other children behave different with familiar and unfamiliar people across settings. There are times when additional observations are needed to see if the child's practical social and community skills are consistent or inconsistent in different settings.

Possible Participation

Parent Issue

My child may have autism as she goes everywhere in the classroom and does not understand how to participate in the classroom activities with other children.

A School Psychologist's Point of View

There are some children who do well in free play or unstructured situations, but have difficulty in structured situations when they are asked to do specific activities. Some children do well in daycare or preschool settings where they can pick or choose their own activities, but struggle in Kindergarten and first grade when more specific tasks are required of them. There are specific teaching strategies and interventions that could help a child who has trouble participating in more structured tasks. Parents may need to be more aware of the type of teacher in a preschool or elementary classroom. For instance, a child who is really disorganized may have difficulty in a classroom where the teacher is disorganized. This same child may respond better to a more structured teaching approach. In a structured approach, the child may learn to participate because the preschool teacher has thought through some of the daily elements in classroom or the preschool setting. The preschool teacher may have carefully organized centers to gain the child's attention and then assist the child by encouraging participation in particular centers. In a structured classroom, a teacher may have a daily schedule to help the young child participate by learning a consistent routine to follow. A preschool or classroom teacher can still individualize a teaching technique or method to address the unique concerns of a child while providing some structure in preschool or classroom setting. Children with autism may need even more structure with visual prompts such as picture cards to choose an activity, posters with pictures of daily tasks or colorful items (colorful folders or tape on floor) to indicate center changes.

Possible Relationship Difficulties

Parent Issue

My young son does not get along well with other children and there always seems to be a disagreement or an issue when he plays with other children.

A School Psychologist's Point of View

When a young child interacts and forms relationships with other children there are varying degrees of the child's behaviors. For example, some children are more social and respond more openly to certain personality types of preschool teachers and children. There are children who respond more openly to other people who have expressive personality types, while some children do better in situations with more reserved and quiet peers and teachers. Different situations, preschool and daycare environments may cause some children to become shy and withdrawn, while other children become more anxious or frustrated in the same environment. There are times when a child may be fearful of another child, an animal, a certain teacher or even a staff worker or volunteer in a day care setting. Sometimes a child has difficulty forming preschool relationships because the child is overly clingy and attached to his or her parent. The child may need time to separate and learn to respond to peers even though the child would prefer to relate only to his or her parent or sibling. There are also times when a child may only partially engage in a relationship. For instance, a child may approach another child only to grab the desired toy and then the sense of a relationship ceases. A child even with autism may approach a parent briefly for food or help with a toy, but not really form a bond or connection that involves turn taking, eye contact and an exchange in a social relationship. Young children with delays in general can also have difficulty forming relationships when they have frustration in learning to share toys and take turns with other children.

Possible Engagement Difficulties

Parent Issue

My son has a difficult time engaging with his preschool teacher when he is approached with activities during the preschool day.

A School Psychologist's Point of View

When young children are approached with direct requests they may engage and respond in different ways. Some children are slow to respond to a request. These children may need time to warm up to the request. Sometimes these children just need to observe the other children around them and they may decide to participate when they see how much fun the other children are having with the activity. There are also children who are very distracted when a request is made by someone. The child may be focused on a toy or curious about an object in a room so he or she ignores the request. Some of these children can be engaged by obtaining his or her attention. A teacher or a therapist may need to say the child's name more than once to secure his or her attention to engage in the game or activity. A child with autism type of characteristics may look away or even turn away when a direct task is given to him or her. Sometimes a child may walk to a corner, get under a table or hide under a desk to avoid the social engagement. Another child may give a blank stare or stare at a toy or object for a while to avoid engagement in activities. Sometimes a child will stare intensely at one toy and it can be difficult to engage and redirect the child away from the toy. Children with engagement difficulties may need different strategies to work on their social engagement skills. A school individualized education plan can have goals to increase social engagement skills at an early age. School staff work who work with the child can develop small goals (small steps) and long term educational objectives. These goals can be refined as progress is made or rewritten if different strategies would be more effective.

Possible Disengagement

Parent Issue

I noticed that my daughter engages in an activity for a few minutes and then disengages or leaves the activity.

A School Psychologist's Point of View

A child may disengage in a structured or unstructured activity for many reasons. For example, a child with a very short attention span may stay with an activity for a few minutes and then get distracted or lose focus with the activity. A child with socialization delays or issues may disengage from a group activity by participating a little while and then withdrawing or becoming anxious during social interaction encounters with other children. Disengagement may also be a sign of autism if the child does not respond to the social cues of those around him or her. If the child avoids eye contact or turns away from a direct request there can be indicators that the child has major deficits in the area of socialization. Often a school psychologist is looking to see if the child is engaging and responding to people and activities around him or her. When a child disengages to the point of being unaware of his or her surroundings, standoffish in large and small group activities and not recognizing others there may be a need to observe the child more or consider if the child has characteristics of autism. Observations by parents, preschool and daycare staff and other professionals working with the child is vital to understanding when a child has disagreements or issues when engaging or disengaging with other children. The big question is whether the child is attempting to communication and socialize with other children or if there is a significant developmental delay, behavioral issue or possible autism when the child shows disengagement or lack of interest in being around other children or adults in social settings.

Possible Lack of Shared Attention

Parent Issue

My son just won't share attention or experiences with me so I think he has something like autism since it is so hard to reach him.

A School Psychologist's Point of View

Parents and professionals will often observe if a child shares a type of joint or shared attention when he or she is approached by someone else. Pre-kindergarten teachers and day care providers can observe this type of shared attention through numerous play experiences between children and interactions with teachers and caregivers who give them requests and directions. It is not uncommon for some young children to just ignore or be un-reactive to some requests. A young child actively playing with a toy train may easily ignore or not focus on a request to clean up or move to a different activity. This lack of joint attention is sometimes related to delayed social skills where the child lacks experiences sharing and taking turns with others. Once the child develops more social interactions with others the joint or shared attention may improve. An 'only child' who is raised primarily by adults may use shared attention with familiar adults, but lack shared attention skills with same age peers and children that are his or her own age. As a child gets older, professionals working with the child are seeing if the shared attention skills are improving or if the child still has difficulty seeing different perspectives that other people bring into situations. Some professionals in the field of autism often encourage the use of turn taking skills for children with autism symptoms. This helps young children learn to shift their attention back and forth with social exchanges for items that involve give and take with others. It is a good start for the child to understand and reach out to others using a concrete item or toy. This simple exchange will hopefully help the child start to initiate more play experiences with other children.

Possible Lack of Interaction

Parent Issue

My daughter doesn't really seem interested in the other children around her at the day care center so I have concerns.

A School Psychologist's Point of View

When children show a lack of interest in others it might be a concern for developmental delays and autism. However, there are different aspects of social interaction that could be considered. A 'flag' for autism is often noted when a child focuses on objects rather than people. In another situation, a child with a possible disability such as a hearing loss may show more interest in playing with an object or toy than the voices and noise around him or her. On the other hand, gifted children or children with higher cognitive abilities may tune out or not socially interact because they are not at the same intellectual level of the children in a preschool setting. On occasion, these children may have temper tantrums or emotional outbursts because the play patterns of the children in a preschool are so varied and the different intellectual abilities of the child. A child with lower cognitive abilities may not know how to ask for help in using or asking for a toy. It is certainly noticed that some children simply do not interact with others because they have communication issues. When a child has not developed a strong vocabulary he or she may not know how to ask for the item that he or she wants to use. This same child could also be unresponsive to social interaction by not responding or acknowledging his or her name when it is called by another child or teacher in a play situation. The lack of social interaction can bring those 'flags' for autism as a young child is observing or playing alone unaware of others. It is important not to mistake a 'shy' child who is introverted or lacks play experiences as having signs of autism

Possible Meaningful Play

Parent Issue

My child can play with many puzzles and objects so I think he has some really good play skills, but his teacher sees this differently.

A School Psychologist's Point of View

A person must really watch and observe the play patterns of a child to see if the child exhibits meaningful play experiences. If a child is exchanging items with another child or able to participate in a 'give or take' or 'back and forth' types of experiences that is wonderful. Some children are delayed in their socialization skills and simply lack play experiences with other children. There are also children with behavioral issues that refuse to share or simply grab a toy or object from another child. Autism concerns can come into play for several reasons. Sometimes a child is over focused on a particular toy that he or she is playing with to the extent that no contact is made with other children or the teacher of a preschool. The child may continue to play directly with the toy being unaware of all the social cues around him or her. There are times when a child appears to be involved in meaningful play on the surface, but the play may actually be more repetitive in nature. For instance, a parent may observe a child putting a puzzle together and think the play is meaningful and appropriate. On the other hand, the parent may miss the cue that the child is doing a repetitive action over and over again as he or she dumps out the puzzle pieces and puts them back in the puzzle many times. Meaningful play involves not only the use of the toy or object, but making an appropriate connection with the use of the toy or object. As play skills increase many children will gain more meaningful experiences by pretending, playing make believe types of games and reaching out to other children for interaction with the toys.

Observations can provide lots of information about meaningful play.

Possible Delayed Response

Parent Issue

My son will not respond to something at first, but later he eventually responds. It is not a fast response and it seems to take him a long time to respond.

A School Psychologist's Point of View

There are some children who at first do not seem to be responsive, but later on show a delayed response. Sometimes people are quick to judge a delayed response as no response. For instance, a person may wave or acknowledge a child and then quickly say a child has no response. However, it may have been that the child was just distracted or amused with a toy, so the response was just delayed. Sometimes a child may not be finished with a task and after the block structure is completed the child will turn and wave (even after the person has left the room). A child may be overly curious about how a toy works so the delayed response to another person may be just a lack of interest in something at a certain time. These delayed responses can be easily misinterpreted as a sign of unresponsiveness. If a child does not respond immediately to a greeting, people may be quick to say the child seems not to hear something. The reality may have been the child hears perfectly fine and eventually responds to others. The request was a delayed response, but was misinterpreted as a child being in his or her 'own world.' Even nonverbal gestures can be delayed. A person may smile at a child and then the child does not immediately smile back so the smile is interpreted as showing a lack of feedback, exchange or social interaction. The child may smile or laugh later about a joke or experience with a delayed type of response. This might mean the child 'got the joke' or 'figured out' the funny saying. I think professionals and families must not forget the importance of these delayed responses, before they think the child has tuned everyone out and shows no response.

Possible Resistance to Change

Parent Issue

My daughter resists change if anyone appears to be leaving the room she is in or going out the front door of the house.

A School Psychologist's Point of View

There are many different scenarios that could impact a child's resistance to change in a home or school setting. For instance, a child who has been neglected may react strongly to someone leaving the home. Sometimes children are so aware of this they may start crying if they see an adult put on a jacket or pick up a purse or brief case. The thought of being neglected again may cause a child to have a strong resistance to change. In school settings this resistance to change often comes when the regular teacher is ill and a substitute may come to change a routine or way something is done in the classroom. Some children respond easily to minor changes, while other children have more resistance to a change in a daily routine. Children with behavioral concerns may be easily annoyed by small changes. Children with autism concerns often resist changes because they have a strong sense of wanting things to be in the same order. A child with autism characteristics can have a major tantrum when someone moves a line up car or only slightly adjusts a lined up object. Some children with autism need a degree of sameness where they are comforted by the objects or toys being put in the same order. When a disruption happens with a change being made, the child will quickly show a side of being inflexible and resistance to any change of a routine. A child with autism concerns who has complicated rituals at home or school will sometimes show some strong resistance or changes in a pattern or routine that is adjusted. It is important to note that resistance to change may or may not be associated with autism so it is wise to really observe the child in changing situations.

Questions to Consider

How can we better inform parents on community resources to increase their parenting skills and strategies?

What are some communication strategies to help children ask for help and assistance?

Where can parents who home school their children get help and extra support for autism and other disorders?

How can educational professionals help children learn to participate in structured and unstructured activities?

What are some fun strategies to engage children in activities and sustain their interest in being around other children?

Additional Autism Exploration Topics

Coping Skills and Autism

Children with Autism and Social Participation

Repetitive Behaviors in the Classroom

Ways to Improve Practical Communication

Helping Children Respond to Direct Requests

Parent Skills to Encourage Child Participation

Assisting Children with Preschool Routines

Autism Classroom Set Up

Building Relationships in an Autism Classroom

Ways to Encourage Meaningful Play

CHAPTER 4

POSSIBLE AUTISM ASPECTS

Chapter four looks at a variety of aspects that could be possible autism. These aspects include a broad range of topics that explore not only a child's interest in a toy or object, but his or her ability to generalize information related to the toy or object. There is interest in how children show reciprocity or a shared interest of the toy with others. There are some children who struggle with inflexibility and have trouble responding to small changes in the order of their play experiences. Not only are professionals observing how the child handles demands, but they are also looking at how the child functions in his or her settings. Some disorders impact a child to a much greater extent than the same disorder in another child who is able to function with less support. Some children can have delayed responses to requests, attention issues, difficulty with joint attention and problems recognizing social cues. There are also children who are selective in how they relate in different situations, preschool or the home setting. Some children will do a task for a familiar person like a parent or family member and would not do the same task if it was requested by an unfamiliar person. There are children who form relationships easily and other children who have trouble forming friendships with other children. There are some children who attempt to communicate and use some social greetings, while other children are distracted and disconnected in some social settings. As well, some children are more aware of the objects in a room than the people surrounding them in the same room or social setting.

Possible Directed Generalization

Parent Issue

My daughter can play with toys and I think that she can even point to a toy so I don't think she has anything like autism.

A School Psychologist's Point of View

There are times parents teach a child to do one thing, but don't go a step further to help the child generalize a skill in a way that could help the child adapt to a school setting. For example, a parent might say point to the red fire truck and the child may go to the red fire truck and point to it, touch it or even pick it up. However, the preschool teacher or elementary teacher may ask the child to point to the red fire truck in a picture book and the child with autism has no idea what the teacher is requesting him or her to do. This can also impact the child in relation to a communication method used in the preschool or classroom. There are children who can name every color on the poster board for the teacher, but when asked to select the 'blue' crayon from the crayon box they have difficulty making a generalization. This is why many teachers use a variety of teaching methods to teach young children in very interactive, hands-on types of classrooms and preschools. A child with autism may be asked to make a choice like choosing a red or blue truck on a picture card. Although the child knows the color red from the fire truck, he or she may not be able to make the choice because it is too difficult for him or her to understand the picture card system used in the classroom. Child with autism and developmental delays may need extra support to help generalize classroom information with real world experiences. Classrooms and preschools that use hands-on practical approaches provide young children with many opportunities to generalize information and use it in many formats, conditions and situations.

Possible Interest

Parent Issue

My son is very interested in playing only with red cars. I. think it shows his preferred interest, but his teacher thinks it might be related to autism.

A School Psychologist's Point of View

Sometimes a child fixates on one element or characteristic of an object and refuses to notice or expand interest in other objects or parts of an object or toy. When this happens the child may be unaware of the purpose or workings of the 'whole object,' because he or she only notices a specific part of a toy or object. This fixation can expand beyond toys and interfere with the child understanding the purpose of a toy or object. For example, a child may constantly fixate or stare at the label on the water bottle without understanding the purpose of drinking water from a bottle. Interest in a particular object may shift from the object to a ritual or repetitive action. Several times I have noticed children staring at water bottles with an amazing interest in my office. Some children seem fascinated by the colorful labels and other children are more interested in the movement of the bottle or how to twist the water bottle cap off. There are so many elements of understanding a child's preferred interest, fascination or just curiosity of a toy or object that makes many parents and professionals have to ask more questions and make more observations to figure out the child's interest in an object. A child playing with red cars, may actually be doing this because of the self stimulation he or she gets from lining up the red cars and not from noticing the features of the red car or interest in how red cars work. On the other hand , children do show preferences for some things and often play hours with a favorite toy or an object that brings them joy. The difference may be a child showing interest in objects or toys versus an extreme fixated interest in one particular object.

Possible Reciprocity

Parent Issue

My child lets all the other kids take his toy and does not interact or approach them about it so I think he has autism problems.

A School Psychologist's Point of View

Reciprocity is described by some professionals as a mutual type of exchange between children with a toy or item. However, reciprocity can be a little more involved for some children. Reciprocity can also be an exchange of information or ideas among children. One child may share information with another and then a teacher may observe the child's response or lack of response to those ideas. A preschool teacher may notice reciprocity related to a safety element. For example, did the child help prevent an accident or redirect another child away from something that was dangerous situation. On a more positive note, reciprocity can be seen as returning a favor or response. One child may smile at another child and that child smiles back as a form of reciprocity. When a child lets other children take his or her toy it can be seen as a sign of several things. On one hand, the child may just lack the social skills or ability to advocate for the use of the toy. The toy can often be taken from this type of child without much response as the child does not understand reciprocity or the exchange of items with another person. On the other hand, a child with autism may show a total lack of reciprocity as he or she ignores all requests to interact, withdraws from many situations and plays by self. This child can show no interest in showing objects or taking objects to others for any type of exchange. Professionals are observing the quality of social reciprocity to see if the child just lacks social or communication skills to exchange or if the child has a strong impairment to avoid multiple attempts to interact and exchange items and ideas.

Possible Inflexibility

Parent Issue

I have autism concerns because my son has to play with household objects in a certain order and get very upset if any objects are moved.

A School Psychologist's Point of View

Parents will sometimes notice inflexibility when a child has behavioral issues. The child may throw a tantrum or have an outburst if a sibling moves a toy or parents accidentally step on a truck. What parents notice first is the inflexibility of the child when only a small change is made in the order of toys or objects. This is different from a child who is casually lining up some ducks or train to play appropriately with toys. It is the intensity of this inflexibility that starts showing red flags for autism. When a child does something very precisely and just explodes if the order is slightly changed, parents start to notice this abnormal type of functioning. Any child may be disappointed if he or she spent hours building a block castle and a sibling knocked it over. A child may naturally protect him or herself from being hurt or to prevent damage to a detailed project. However, a child with autism characteristics may become overly upset with only the slightest alteration of something. This reaction to the disruption of the order of something becomes a strong source of agitation for the child who almost calms him or herself by putting an object or toy in a ritualistic order. Sometimes these rituals by the child start out simple and become more complicated. The child is inflexible if an object is overturned or moved away. Although the child may be totally unaware of the people and social situation of the room, the child is very aware of the ritualistic and repetitive nature of objects. Inflexibility is certainly an autism concern because it entails that awareness of objects in a rigid way where the child is unable to function in a world where positions, movement and change are constantly happening.

Possible Functional Impact

Parent Issue

I think my child needs to be in an autism program because he flaps his hands when excited and this is something my friends have noticed.

A School Psychologist's Point of View

Many times school professionals and community mental health workers are looking to see if the child's symptoms impact how he or she functions in home, school or community settings. There are some children where there is an appearance of functioning well at times, but at other times the child has difficulty functioning in certain situations. For instance, a child may find his or her way around a small school, but who can't function at all in a larger school with a higher population of students. A child may be able to find the cafeteria when there are supportive teachers directing him or her down the hall, but when that support is missing on a certain day the child doesn't function as well and gets lost or sidetracked trying to get to the cafeteria. Anytime a routine is slightly changed or altered the child must make an adjustment or adaptation to the change and some children can function with the change, while other children have difficulties with the change. Some children have such mild symptoms that even though they are classified with having autism or another disorder, they can actually function well in a regular education setting with minimal support. Other children have a much greater need for support and need a more structured program to help function in the daily setting. Many professionals are looking at the functional impact the disorder has on the child's educational and social life. Some children will need more services as the functional impact of a disorder could cause the child distress and tension, while another child may need minimal assistance as the child functions fairly well in various settings.

Possible Demands

Parent Issue

My daughter does fine in free play, but she has trouble responding to any type of demand placed on her by her teachers.

A School Psychologist's Point of View

The area of demands is very interesting in the field of child development. There are times when a child has major behavior and control issues that come out when a child has demands placed on him or her. Demands are presented to children in different ways. Sometimes the youngest child in a family may insist that everyone bring him or her food so that he just points or gestures and the older siblings bring his or her requested item. However, when a child wants something in a preschool setting and is encouraged to use words for a request a tantrum may break out because the child's personal demands were not met in the way he or she expected. The environment does impact the type of demands put on a child. For example, a preschool with a day of unstructured free play types of activities will get different responses from some children than a structured, very routine preschool with an ordered set of activities. Demands may change as the child goes to a higher grade in elementary school. There may be no problems in preschool with more unstructured activities, but as the child gets older and has more demands placed on him or her in kindergarten and first grade other issues related to demands become more evident. There may be more tantrums, frustration and the child may lack the capabilities to function in a very demanding environment. Demands are not always strong and sometimes a simple direct request for the child seems like a big demand of pressure for the child. Professionals may need to help the child develop strategies to deal with more demands. These professionals will look to see how the demands impact the child's functioning in school and home situations.

Possible Delayed Engagement

Parent Issue

My daughter seems to withdraw from some things and then starts to engage later-is this something like autism?

A School Psychologist's Point of View

Many children are slow to warm up and engage in activities. At first glance, these children seem withdrawn, disinterested and totally disengaged in tasks and activities. A child with autism may also turn away from many attempts to engage or participate in a direct request. There have been situations where a child with autism takes a puzzle, turns away and sits under a desk or in a corner with puzzles or blocks. These children may complete the task, but do not engage in the social part of the activity. A child with social delays may not engage quickly, but then warm up to a social situation and participate. There are some children who are very selective in the activities they choose to engage in as part of social settings. A child may refuse all activities where a direct request is made and only play with toys or a preferred interest. Some children will then leave the toys and come to the testing table to draw a picture or build with blocks in a structured activity. There are some children who will not participate for the first 30 minutes and then engage in the later part of an activity. This delayed engagement may also be related to how familiar the child is working with the adult who is making the request. A child may complete a request only from his or her mother or father, but ignore all requests from therapists, teachers and caregivers who work with the child. Some children won't engage with certain adults, but then engage easily with a different person. Comfort level may certainly play a role in engagement activities and when a child has warmed up in some settings this can impact if the child has a delayed engagement with communication and social situations.

Possible Attention

Parent Issue

My daughter does not always respond to requests and focuses attention elsewhere-is this something that kids with autism might do?

A School Psychologist's Point of View

Attention to tasks and people is a big question to ask when looking at developmental delays and autism. There are children who get distracted very easily by toys and other items and it is difficult to gain their attention. Some children get distracted a little, but take redirection and will focus their attention on a task. There are some children who have a delayed response when others are seeking their attention. A child's name may have be called three or four times before the child's attention is gained. If there are autism concerns a team may look to see if the child's attention is gained from pointing to objects or making eye contact to designate the desire to obtain an object. Attention may be noticed through the child's social interaction with others. For example, a child may show attention for a toy or person by demonstrating that he or she has a social smile with others and in doing certain activities. Another important element of attention is looking at the child's ability and willingness to show joint attention toward an object or person. In play, a school psychologist or therapist may notice if the child can focus attention during a fun game or task or if the child will show attention during a pretend activity. A multidisciplinary-team assessing a young child may also look to see if the child shows attention to acknowledge a person with a social greeting when entering or leaving a room. Different professionals will notice various things about how the child's attention can be gained as they are looking at different aspects of the child in terms of medical, psychological, motor, communication and other skills. Attention is a broad area and can encompass a number of autism and non-autism features.

Possible Joint Attention

Parent Issue

My child can't seem to hold his attention on anything and just moves from toy to toy in the preschool he has been attending.

A School Psychologist's Point of View

The world of 'attention' can include many different things. Sometimes school professionals are observing the child to see if he or she can focus on an activity or task long enough to understand what is happening. A speech therapist may look to see if the child displays a joint attention when completing a task or responding to another person joint referencing types of skills. For example, a professional can consider if the child can respond on his or her own or if the child can respond with prompting or to see if the child simply gives no response or reaction to the attention of an object or person. A professional may ask, does the child put words together to gain attention or is the child just using spontaneous words with no attention or direction? Professionals are often looking at two different things related to joint attention. First, is the child's attention related to his or her own awareness of what is going on around him or her or reaching out to be aware of others in social settings? This may be a child staring blankly or giving all of his or her visual attention to only one detail or particular toy with the exclusion of other class activities or human interactions going on in the preschool or classroom. Finally, professionals are also watching the child's attention to tasks to observe pragmatic or practical skills. This can often be easily observed in the toy center when sharing becomes an issue of concern. A professional will look to see if the child uses his or her attention to 'give and take' items and reach out to others for social interaction or if the child struggles to understand the practical issues of this type of social interaction.

Possible Social Cues

Parent Issue

My son just seems to be in his own inner world and does not respond to people making a remark or reaching out with a social cue.

A School Psychologist's Point of View

A child who does not respond to social cues may lack a variety or communication and social skills. This is why observation of the child's behavior is social situations is so important in determining if a child shows autism characteristics or other types of delays. If a child is not responding to a social cue by withdrawing it could be a sign of possible depression as the child shows a lack of interest in fun and enriching activities with other children. There can be signs of anxiety in a child who cannot respond or function in a social setting where he or she may feel distressed. Sometimes a child does not respond to a social cue because he or she lacks the communication skills or vocabulary to answer a social or verbal request. A child with autism characteristics may be fearful of a social situation or withdraw when approached with a social request. The child could respond to a social cue with an inappropriate action such as laughing when something is not funny or staring off when social interaction is taking place. This inappropriate response can sometimes be a reaction to not understanding a social cue or simply not knowing how to respond to a social cue by a person who surprises the child with some request or saying that seems uncomfortable. The child may not know how to react appropriately to a social cue so the child may comfort him or herself by doing something repetitively like turning on and off the lights or running back and forth across the room. A number of children comfort themselves with movement activities and the motion of different movements may help them to relax or deal with stressful situations in response to the social cues around them.

Possible Selective Relationships

Parent Issue

My son will do things for me, but not for anyone else. I guess he is just more familiar with me so I can get him to go some things he won't do for his preschool teacher.

A School Psychologist's Point of View

Professionals will quickly notice how a child reacts to different people as he or she forms a relationship or social bonds with others. Almost immediately, a child who is overly clingy to his parents will be hard to engage in many activities away from the parent. However, some children are clingy to the parent at first, but then become engaged in activities after a 'warming up' period of time. Parents will also share when a child seems unattached to them. A parent may tell how a child will go off with anyone in a store and not recognize stranger types of danger at all. The child may separate from the parent and go with other people never looking back to check with his or her parent. Children from the foster care system may desire attachment and quickly hug or become affectionate with people they hardly know. There are other children with high levels of risk taking behaviors that go right up to people without any sense of danger or safety. Children with autism characteristics sometimes show difficulties in forming relationships with other people. Professionals will be looking to see if children can develop relationships in different social experiences whether at home or in a preschool environment. A professional may look to see if the child is starting to form friendships through play experiences. The child may be selective in at times showing a preference for playing with certain friends, attach to some children in small group situations or reacting positively or negatively when in a large group setting. The professionals will look to see if the child reacts differently to various personality types and can adjust his or her behavior to different people and experiences.

Possible Communication Attempts

Parent Issue

My son talks to other children, so I don't think he has autism. I mean he can communicate with some children and I think that is enough.

A School Psychologist's Point of View

In looking at whether a child has autism or developmental delays professionals are often observing how a child is using language by directing it to others and responding to the language of others. If a child uses words randomly with no real coordinated effort to respond to something or someone then I would be more likely to suspect possible autism characteristics. However, when a child comments about other students in the preschool class, I have a tendency to look more toward developmental delays because he or she is showing an awareness of others. For example, a young boy in an autism classroom immediately notices another student putting rocks in his mouth. The child goes to the teacher assistant and says 'he's eating rocks" as he points to the other little boy. This same child goes to another student and says 'it's not cool to eat rocks' and 'don't eat rocks.' This is an example of a child is using language to communicate a concern to other people and this is a 'purposeful' attempt to use language. The teacher may even look at this child making all of these communication attempts and wonder if this child really has autism or possibly just developmental delays. The above example is quite different than a child who is just babbling to make sounds over and over again without a communicative intent. There are times when children will make attempts to communicate only personal needs, but not make communicative attempts at other times. For instance a child may say 'juice' or take the parent's hand to touch the juice as a communicative intent, but won't ask for a toy or an object that is high on a shelf in another situation.

Possible Social Greeting

Parent Issue

My daughter uses social greetings, but my family still thinks that she really has autism. I mean she uses social greetings everyday when I leave for work.

A School Psychologist's Point of View

As a school psychologist, I often observe a child's use of social greetings to see if the social greeting is initiated by the child or if prompting is needed or the child is just repeating a request from a prompt or reminder. As well, some children have memorized a social greeting and say phrases in a rote type of way like 'how are you' or 'come on in.' There are some parents who misinterpret social greetings as appropriate when the child is just repeating a phrase he or she has heard others use in social settings. A child may say 'good morning to you' as you enter the room, but make no further interaction with the social greeting. The phrase may just be a repeated phrase the child has memorized and will use over and over again. At first, the social greeting will almost seem appropriate, but other social interaction with the person will be very limited or almost nonexistence. On the other hand, a child without prompting who says 'what's your name' or 'why are you here' can be showing a social awareness to greet or approach another person.

Often a child who initiates a social greeting to someone else might also be making eye contact and reaching out in an attempt to communicate. The social greetings are interesting to observe in young children because this area can really show the difference of a child using rote type social greetings versus a child using a social greeting to make an attempt to communicate and socially interact with others. Most parents and professionals encourage children to use social greetings, but the child's perspective of using a social greeting as a practical exchange with another person is quite different from a repeated social greeting with little meaning.

Possible Disconnection

Parent Issue

My child seems disconnected from other children and activities at playgroup and I think she might have autism.

A School Psychologist's Point of View

Parents and teachers may observe a child being disconnected from classroom, preschool or home activities. This could be a sign the child is delayed in many areas. For example, a child who has low cognitive or intellectual abilities may not make connections between toys or items presented to him or her and become frustrated or confused. He or she may not understand how groups of objects are connected or logically presented. On the other hand, a child with a short attention span may disconnect by losing interest in an activity or being totally unorganized with the materials or the major point of the activity. Young children with autism can often show signs of disconnecting to activities. For instance, a preschool filled with toys and wonderful educational materials may barely be noticed by some children with possible autism. The child may go from toy to toy with no intended purpose or simply avoid the toys all together and head to the teacher's desk to climb up and touch the computer keys. The child may pull items such as paper or folders off a shelf with no intended purpose. This disconnection makes teaching skills somewhat difficult for preschool teachers and caregivers. A simple request to clean up or pick up toys can become a mess as a child puts toys in a tub and then pours the toys out as he or she repeats the activity many times. Parents and professionals soon notice this is not just a playing game, but rather a disconnection between the child understanding the clean up task. Professionals and educators are often observing for some type of connection or some type of logical arrangement of how toys or items are presented together in a connecting format.

Possible Distraction

Parent Issue

My son is so distracted he never stays on any task. It is almost like he never stays with a toy to see how it even works.

A School Psychologist's Point of View

Childhood distractions can fall into many different areas. There are times a child has a short attention span and only stays with an activity for a short period of time before being distracted by toys and items in the classroom. For other children distractions are more complicated. A child with autism may be so distracted that the child develops a 'ritualistic' type of behavior. The child may not play with any item for an extended period of time and then take every toy off of the shelf with no purpose in playing with the toys. Some parents will say that child does this distracting type of behavior every time the child goes to a new place and some parents don't view this as a distraction, but think of it as appropriate play. Distractions from tasks impact children in school because of missing assignments, incomplete projects and lack of task completion. The parent will want to address the challenges of a child who is overly distracted by possibly working with early childhood intervention specialists and school staff to find out strategies or methods that work best for the child. Teachers working with child on a daily basis can often come up with some reinforcements or strategies to help the child with distractions. There may be organizational strategies if the child has attention deficit issues. A child with autism may need specific behavioral strategies to help the child develop appropriate skills to deal with distraction and task avoidance. Sometimes a home based type of educational plan is developed to help the child with distractions. In the preschool or school setting, goals may be developed to modify the learning environment and support responses to distractions.

Possible Awareness of Objects

Parent Issue

My child seems to notice small details about objects and this extreme awareness of objects is bothersome to me.

A School Psychologist's Point of View

A child who has a very detailed awareness of objects may appear in different ways. For example, a child who notices his name was left off the board for centers may be pointing out to the teacher that he or she overlooked his or her name. However, a child who makes a big deal over very small details may show an obsessive concern for an object. A child who says 'my cabin' over and over again because he or she notices it was not on the bulletin board and then gets panicked because his cabin name sticker is not on the board may just need reassurance that it is no big deal. In terms of autism, this may be an indication that a child has some possible autism characteristics. The child may be repetitively asking about something on the bulletin board or in the room or get really upset if an object or picture is moved out of order and not precisely where it should be. This can be related to how the child socially interacts as well as stereotyped or repetitive types of behaviors related to a social or classroom situation. For instance, preschool classrooms and school rooms are often theme based so bulletin boards and classroom decorations may change monthly or seasonally. Some children with delays and possible autism may not notice this change at all, while other children may acknowledge the change and then adjust to the new classroom situation. There may be some children in the classroom with very restricted interests that this change and awareness of new objects presents difficulty for them. Teachers, parents and caregivers may need to acknowledge these changes and address why the change was made in the preschool or school setting.

Questions to Consider

How can we help children to respond more often to demands or requests to participate in activities?

What are some ways to encourage children to be more flexible and play with a variety of toys rather than one specific toy?

When children are disconnected from activities, what are some things we can consider to help connect them in an educational setting?

How can staff workers help a child who is distracted stay on a specific task?

What are some ways to help children participate in reciprocal (shared) play with other children?

Additional Autism Exploration Topics

Expanding a Child's Interest in Different Topics

Helping Children Gain Flexibility Skills

Coping with Changes in School Settings

Strategies to Recognize Social Cues

Sharing Skills and Autism

Preferred versus Non-Preferred Interests

How to Increase Toy Exchange

Autism Functioning in the Community

Helping Children with Demanding Behavior

Gaining a Child's Attention

CHAPTER 5

POSSIBLE AUTISM INDICATORS

The final chapter of autism indicators emphasizes that there is a degree of uncertainty with some autism issues. There can be questions regarding a child's eligibility related to autism. These questions and indicators often surround possible signs, symptoms and risk factors related to autism. Some of the indicators point toward suspicion of autism and sometimes they don't point in that direction. It is important to note that professionals have different perspectives about autism, delays and disorders and sometimes parents need additional information or to be redirected to other resources in the community. These signs and symptoms are sometimes misread or misjudged by parents and professionals. As a result, children with autism concerns may be misplaced or put in a mismatched program. It is somewhat complicated because parents are bombarded with 'red flags' of autism symptoms that overlay or mimic other associated conditions. Professionals may misinterpret social cues and children may present with variations of autism and other disorders ranging from mild to severe conditions. As a result, parents have many questions for preschool and school staff about the child's placement and interventions used to help the child. The one thing many professionals are looking for is the quality of the child's actions when he or she is communicating and interacting in a social setting. Observation is a key component in looking at the quality of the child's actions. This helps in determining if the child has possible autism or other developmental delays or conditions that might present for the child's educational eligibility.

Possible Eligibility

Parent Issue

My son was found eligible as a student with autism, but his teacher questions if he has autism from her classroom observations.

A School Psychologist's Point of View

Unfortunately, some professionals may have determined that a child has met an autism eligibility without enough evidence or documentation about the child's behaviors or characteristics of autism. A short half day or less assessment of a child, may not (in some cases) provide a complete picture of how a child communicates and socially interacts with others. As a result, the child goes out into an autism classroom and teachers as well as other professionals start to see the child does have the ability to communicate his or her needs and socialize with a few strategies. A good start is for the parent to consult with the teacher, speech therapist and school psychologist to share and receive the feedback about the child. The parent then can revisit the individualized education plan and see if the special education placement is appropriate for the child or if other strategies or modifications could be implemented. Professionals can vary in their opinions on this matter. For example, some school psychologists don't always want to change an eligibility of autism, but might be more willing to change placement options. On the other hand, some multidisciplinary teams at schools are more than willing to change an eligibility category or exit a child from a program if an eligibility category was inaccurate or did not describe the needs and abilities of the child. Eligibility can be a little tricky in that states may have different guidelines and approaches for determining if a child is eligible for special education services.

One state might suggest a child needs services for deficit areas without identifying an eligibility category, while another state may have a very specific eligibility category

Possible Symptoms

Parent Issue

My daughter may have autism because she is restless and tantrums everyday. I am not sure about her symptoms.

A School Psychologist's Point of View

There are times when a symptom is mentioned and then there is an immediate suspicion of autism. However, it is important to look at the full picture of the child and notice that some symptoms are also obvious for other disorders. For example, a child who is restless and irritable may also have an anxiety disorder. Children who have difficulty concentrating or are easily distracted may have attention problems. A child with trust issues may be experiencing an attachment type of disorder. Tantruming is often noticed in very young children struggling with language and communication delays. Once some children increase their vocabulary and can express wants and needs better the tantrums sometimes decrease. A tantrum can also be related to a child who is overwhelmed with emotion and may possibly have a type of mood disorder. However, when a child shows no emotion and has difficulty with social reciprocity and social exchanges there may be more characteristics of autism presented in the child. Professionals are often looking to see if the child shows deficits in communication and social interaction in different social contexts. A symptom may not show in one setting, but be very prevalent in another situation or different social setting. The symptom may come out with a particular person and then not show itself when other people are around the child. These symptoms can be observed through body language, use of gestures, play responses, back and forth turn taking, responses to requests from teachers, parents and caregivers as well as how the child engages and initiates conversations with others.

Possible Signs

Parent Issue

My child just has a few autistic signs, but she doesn't actually have autism and this is really confusing for our family.

A School Psychologist's Point of View

There are some parents and professionals who do not want to actually come out and say that a child has autism or autism characteristics. Some parents will not even mention that their child has a diagnosis of autism to the school district staff. I am not sure if this is just an avoidance or way to just ignore autism concerns in the hope that the child will 'grow out' of these signs and symptoms or if parents think another team will go a different direction for the child. Professionals can also cast doubts about autism when they put in their reports phrases like 'a stigmata of autism,' 'an impression of some autism signs' or 'shows mild characteristics of autism.' These types of phrases often leave parents in doubt as to whether the child actually has autism or if there is just a speculation that a child has a possibility of having autism. There are parents who will comment that one professional tells them one thing about the child and another professional told them something totally different. The parents then come to an assessment with their arms in the air, saying they have no idea if the child has autism or not because they have been told so many different things by various people. If there are major doubts about the signs of autism, then there may be a need for more observation, interviews and discussions about how the child behaves, interacts in social situations and communicates with the people around him or her. The important point to remember is that the educational professionals need to develop a full, well documented picture of the child in order to start forming a plan to help the child succeed in an appropriate educational setting.

Possible Risks

Parent Issue

Someone said my child has a 'risk for autism'-does that mean she really has autism or should I just forget about this?

A School Psychologist's Point of View

Sometimes we here the term 'at risk of developing...' This may come from an autism screening instrument that recognized some 'red flags' or 'signs of autism.' There are some instruments that even describe the risk with varying degrees such as a 'low risk' for autism or a 'greater risk' for autism based on certain questions and how they were answered. It is important to remember that a 'risk of developing something' does not always mean that a child will get a disorder. Many medical disorders suggest that some children with certain diseases are at risk for having an intellectual disability or a learning disability. Some children develop learning problems and some do not have any intellectual difficulties or learning setbacks. Some children who are adopted will often have a statement in various reports that they are at risk of developing emotional problems or mental illness based on family information. Some of these adopted children are fine, while others struggle more with emotional issues. At various points in foster care experiences some children have experiences with both positive role models and possible negative experiences that may influence the number of risk factors the child is facing in life. There are also children that are at risk for having developmental delays. Some children may not be delayed at all when they are very young, but could be delayed as academics speed up in the early grades. When a child is viewed as 'at risk for developing autism' a full assessment is needed to determine if the child has communication and socialization deficits, repetitive or restrictive interests or possible delays that are impacting his or her educational progress.

Possible Perspectives

Parent Issue

I think my child is just a little shy around new people and this bothers my husband-is there a chance my son has autism?

A School Psychologist's Point of View

There are times when parents don't see any of the child's behaviors or actions as atypical or different. Sometimes this happens because parents just get used to a child's 'way of acting' and it starts to seem typical to them. An example of this might be a child who is constantly crawling under the tables. The speech therapist, nurse and school psychologist may view the child's behavior as a refusal to complete tasks, defiant behavior and a child wanting to do things on his or her own terms. The parent may view the child as 'shy and a little withdrawn' around new people. Of course, autism concerns would come up as he or she crawls under table because the child is being 'standoffish' from those around him or her. The child might be avoiding eye contact, resisting contact with people and not being aware of his or her surroundings. Another perspective could easily be that the child is refusing the request to come out from under the table because he or she wants to be control of the situation and will come out when he or she is ready and on his own terms. What is tricky for many people looking at autism is that a child may respond to some communication and social requests appropriately and other social interaction and communication requests inappropriately. This is a concern, however the child will have some strengths and weaknesses that could be worked on as interventions in the school setting. If there is uncertainty about the child's actions then more observations should be completed to obtain additional information on how the child responds to various requests and tasks presented by different people in a variety of settings.

Possible Program Mismatch

Parent Issue

My child is really bright and has had discipline issues at three charter schools-could all of these problems possibly be autism?

A School Psychologist's Point of View

There are some children who exhibit social issues because the school or educational program does not fit their needs. The student may withdraw or even become aggressive toward others because he or she is not challenged or gets bored with the school activities. There is what I call the 'gifted issue' and that is that very bright children with higher cognitive abilities may look at times like they have some autism characteristics because they sometimes 'think' outside of the box and look at learning differently than other children in classrooms. Teachers who have not worked with gifted and extremely bright children may not catch these unusual patterns of learning and different styles of learning taking place in a classroom. As a result, the teacher may overlook some unique and curious aspects of the child or mistake them for autism characteristics. Some children have moved around from school to school so there is no long tern documentation of strategies that have worked with the child. If no interventions have been tried then it is hard to determine if the child's behavior may change or improve from a particular strategy or teaching method. At times, behaviors like withdrawal, lack of eye contact or avoiding a speaker may mimic autism when these behaviors are really a child who yearns for something more. The child may really just desire to be challenged and find a niche for his or her creative outlet or a way to express strong cognitive abilities in a school or educational setting that does not provide that enrichment. Parents working with teaching and school staff can help open the door to communication to address these legitimate educational concerns.

Possible Misread Actions

Parent Issue

My daughter sometimes has a strange habit. She moves her arms around and around for no reason. This is something I am watching.

A School Psychologist's Point of View

I think parents and professionals must be cautious not to read too much into a particular action without fully studying the mannerisms of the child. I once noticed a little boy on an airplane who presented as have fairly good social and communication skills. He would make eye contact, be aware of other people on the plane and make his parents aware of his need to go to the bathroom or get out of the airplane seat. He did have one unusual habit and that was he often put his hands in a circular pattern. At first, as I observed him my first thought was this might be autism. However, then I noticed he only put his hands in the circular pattern when he was nervous or anxious. When he had to wait to go to the bathroom as another person was in the bathroom he would put his hands around and around in the circular motion. When the plane took off and landed he would do the circular pattern with his hands. My thoughts in observing this child were quickly focused on the anxiety and nervousness he presented when in certain stress situations. However, when not in a stressful situation, his behavior seemed typical and appropriate for a child his age. This cue of repetitively putting his hands in a circular motion could be read by some professionals as a sign of autism. However, my experience indicated that this would probably be a misread signal with a stronger indication of some possible anxiety or nervousness for the child in some situations. Sometimes the rush to come up with a conclusion for the child's behavior is misread with quick decisions. Professionals must look at the whole picture of the child and strive not to misread a child's action in a single particular situation.

Possible Misjudging of Signs

Parent Issue

My son moves so fast he darts around the room very quickly like he might have something like autism. I want to get this checked out.

A School Psychologist's Point of View

Signs of autism must be viewed with caution in order to look at the whole picture of the child. For instance, many young children dart quickly down the hall and rush to the playground and present as high energy children. Even some children with autism dart down the hall, but the difference may be that they may run back and forth in a repetitive motion or show a lack of awareness of being quiet in the hallway. I have observed parents who mistake hand flapping for hand tremors. There have also been parents who overlook 'hand flapping' and say the child is just 'waving' his or her hands. Sometimes a parent denies an autism characteristics by saying the child is not flapping hands, but he or she is just jumping up and down. Autism signs can be misread or misjudged if a person sees different things. A school psychologist may ask a parent if the child calls other children names and some parents will respond the child is calling 'bad names to others.' Some parents misinterpret that question by saying 'yes' he or she can call the name of his or her friend or brothers and sister. A parent may say the child knows the name of his or her brother or sister or can call out the names of his or her cousins and older children or relatives in the family. One parent viewed 'name calling' as a positive type of trait, while the other parent might view 'name calling' as a naughty type of provoking behavior. Signs must be viewed with the whole child in mine to get a look at his or her strengths and weaknesses. This allows professionals and parents to see if there are many signs of autism or just particular isolated behavior issues.

Possible Red Flags

Parent Issue

My child's teacher says he has some 'red flags' for autism and I am not really sure how to react to this information.

A School Psychologist's Point of View

Parents shouldn't immediately be alarmed by 'red flags' or possible indications of autism, developmental delays or other conditions. Sometimes a teacher observes something during the day as a child plays in the center and just suggests to the parents to consider getting the child 'checked out.' There are times these 'red flag' concerns turn out to be nothing and at other times a delay, concern or disorder is noted by the professional observing the child. Occasionally, a professional will note a very unusual occurrence and may even recommend a genetic referral or further testing. Sometimes a medical condition is noted by a nurse as part of the multi-team assessment and the red flag may actually turn out to be a medical condition rather than autism. There are other times the 'red flag' just indicates possible delays and then the assessment team will note if there are actual delays or if the child is on target in various areas of development. Red flags can also come from a child who lacked experience and nurturing as a very young child. A child with an unstable early home environment may or may not present with red flags or at risk types of symptoms. However, a 'red flag' could be noted in the preschool and may warrant additional monitoring or testing. It is important to note that even some children have 'red flags' there are some of these children who become like sponges and start to blossom and grow quickly when placed in an enriching and stable educational environment. Other children may have more difficulty in coping with change and their 'red flags' may present as more serious conditions that need a higher level of support in an educational setting.

Possible Associated Conditions

Parent Issue

My daughter may have autism, but I really think that she is just inattentive and may have some type of attention disorder.

A School Psychologist's Point of View

There are some children who have clear cut symptoms of autism, while other children are more complex and may have associated disorders. There are a wide range of deficits children can have with or without autism and as a result it is sometimes difficult to determine how much support a child will need. In the same way, some children may have more severe symptoms of autism and associated disorders, while other children seem to function more on the mild side. In addition, a particular symptom may require more intensive interventions for the child, while another child only needs limited support or simply a monitoring or consultation type of approach. For instance, a child with repetitive behavioral patterns may need a different strategy at home than the one that works in the school setting. A child's interest in a topic may be focused differently in a community setting instead of a school setting. Children with autism can have stronger deficits in one area over another. Changes are being made in diagnostic manuals and guidelines to better describe some symptoms to have more accuracy in describing the symptoms and conditions of the child. Sometimes a child is better described as having autism, but at other times developmental delays are more prevalent. There are some children better described as having a medical condition, a mental disorder or genetic considerations. In the same way a child with autism may or may not have a cognitive or language impairment. There is a need to explore how these associated conditions, disorders and the child's symptoms relate to how the child functions at school, home and in the community.

Possible Symptom Overlap

Parent Issue

My daughter does some things that seem autistic and other things that appear to be normal or typical for her age.

A School Psychologist's Point of View

There are many times when disorders or symptoms seem to overlap and that makes determining educational eligibilities difficult for many professionals. Sometimes symptoms or signs are seen across settings by various individuals working with a child and at other times symptoms are sporadic as they appear different in various settings. A child may challenge parents more at home, but be a doll and well behaved at school. On the other hand, a child may be wonderful at home without demands and a challenge at school when classroom rules and demands are placed on him or her. A child who is anxious or nervous may be unresponsive when his or her name is called. He or she may avoid eye contact or fail to react to others in a room as a response to being anxious or nervous. The child may appear to have autism signs, but what might be happening is that the so-called signs of autism may actually be anxiety or another disorder that overlaps some symptoms of autism. In an educational assessment, a team is not diagnosing a disorder, but looking to see if the child meets the requirements of a particular special education category or specific eligibility. In terms of describing a child and developing an educational plan, the team of professionals and parents are looking at the best way to describe the child's symptoms, strengths and weaknesses and then develop an educational plan to meet his or her educational needs.

There are differences and some states are more specific about describing the child than other states. Some states just explain the child's deficits and put the child in a program, while other states have more specific eligibility categories.

Possible Misinterpretations

Parent Issue

One person made the comment that 'my child might have autism,' but the other professionals seem to disagree.

A School Psychologist's Point of View

There are times when professionals misinterpret the child's social cues for various reasons. For example, a teacher doing an intake and spending only a few minutes with a child may say 'he's not making eye contact- it could be autism.' However, when the school psychologist and speech therapist work for longer periods of time with the child they may discover that the child warms up, starts making eye contact and shows a greater participation to complete tasks. It is easy for one professional to make a quick interpretation of a child's characteristic or cue. There are times when a child may have multiple sensory issues and some unusual behaviors as a result of a possible vision or hearing disorder. At times additional testing may need to be done before a vision or hearing impairment can be considered because there is a lack of documentation to specifically identify the impairment. Professionals do have different ideas about children based on their training and experiences. It is good for parents to hear some different perspectives about the child, but they should try to focus back on the child's personal needs and strengths.. However, professionals need to be cautious and take more time to observe the child and see if the child's cues and responses were documented and detailed, rather than a quick judgment call based on very limited information. The parent may need to explore more of the characteristics of autism and see if those characteristics describe his or her child's actions or behaviors. A misinterpretation by a professional could steer a family in the wrong direction for resources and overlook other delays, possible disorders or conditions of the child.

Possible Variations

Parent Issue

My child may have autism, so is there anything I could do to help her with these challenges and difficulties. I really need more information.

A School Psychologist's Point of View

Autism impacts children in different ways and so children don't all appear to respond in the same way. As a result, some therapies and approaches may help some children while other children do not respond to them. Parents may try special diets and some of these improve the child's behavior and other children with autism do not respond to these diets. There have been parents who indicate success with a particular preschool program, but there is not always extensive documentation of these programs, but rather just parent testimonials. Parents involved in their child's education may see things that work for a particular child with an approach or program, but this may not transfer to other children with different needs. I guess it would make sense that children with varying severity levels of autism may use therapy, modification, diet and other approaches that would need to be individualized. An approach can be very helpful to one child who responds well to a therapy, while another child with different issues does not respond at all to a particular approach or therapy. If a child has some deficits or weaknesses in one area and another child has different deficits and concerns it would make sense that a very individualized approach should be used with each child. Parents and professionals see that some approaches have been studied more often and have a stronger basis or foundation for their claims, while other approaches may be new and lack a less established track record for helping children with autism. Variations of treatments for each educational approach with a child should be taken in consideration of how the child functions in both home and school settings.

Possible Placement Options

Parent Issue

My child can't have autism because I can't afford to send him to a special school that is very expensive. Are there any other options for me to consider?

A School Psychologist's Point of View

There are times when parents hear the word 'autism' at an eligibility meeting and many ideas start running through their heads. A parent may have a strong reaction to autism because the parent thought the child would not be able to attend the same private school with his or her older sister. Parents from different countries can remember friends who paid thousands of dollars for an autism program to help the child, so the parents assume they will have to pay for a program in the public schools in a different country. At other times, parents can be adamant that a child stays in his or her same preschool even if the preschool does not offer special education or anyone working specifically in the area of autism. Parents may want or desire a child with special needs to be placed in a private school setting without fully checking out the private school to see if there are special education or specialized programs that would meet the child's needs. There is often a need to really spend time and explain that the educational needs of the child come first. Some educational environments work better for some children than other types of educational settings. Parents also need to be aware that special education program placements in a school or other settings can change if the child's skills improve and if they start needing more support or supervision. Parents also need to inform the school of any medical changes or major disruptions in a child's life that may impact behavior or academic performance in the school setting.

Educational placement in special education programs can change if the child makes progress or has setbacks in relations to his or educational goals and objectives.

Possible Interventions

Parent Issue

My child may have autism, but the school he attends won't test him until he has had some type of interventions.

A School Psychologist's Point of View

It is unfortunate that some students are overlooked or not evaluated for autism and other disorders because the 'intervention' system of a school district may fail to identify the need for an assessment. Parents have shared stories that children start the intervention process and then the teacher leaves and the new teacher or long term substitute teacher does not finish implementing the interventions for the child. Sometimes a school team is responsible for the paperwork of the child going through the intervention process and the documentation of the interventions is not completed. At other times, the child moves to a new school and the intervention records from the previous school are not forwarded to the new school. Another scenario could be a child who is very transient and moves from school to school. This child could have had numerous interventions stopped and started without getting a complete picture of the child's deficits or strengths. There are times when parents pull the child from a public school with a bad experiences and then home school the child. A child in this home school situation may be overlooked for both interventions and consideration of an assessment for autism and other delays or disorders. The key to understanding interventions is communication among the professionals working with the child to share information, observations and experiences that explain the child's responses, reactions and deficits related to the areas of academics, communication and social experiences and capabilities. This information can be very helpful for determining the child's educational eligibility and placement in an appropriate program.

Possible Quality

Parent Issue

Should I be concerned because my son has a funny way that he 'waves?' The speech therapist says he is hand flapping, but I am just not sure.

A School Psychologist's Point of View

School psychologists and educational professionals are often looking at the quality of the child's behaviors, reactions and responses in relation to autism and other delays or disorders. There is a big difference in a child who 'waves' and responds to the social greeting of 'bye' and the child who is continually 'hand flapping' being unaware of his or her surroundings. What is different is the interpretation by parents, professionals and those working with the child on the child's actions. Parents may start to recognize if the child has to constantly have reminders to complete a task or if the child develops a spontaneity to seek out activities and become more independent as he or she initiates activities and seeks the attention of others. Professionals may notice if the child's quality of play involves turn taking, reciprocal interaction, gazing responses to others or the use of gestures to stop or start a social exchange. The quality of a child's responses is one indication of whether the child is responding adequately to tasks or if there is a deficit, lack of understanding or delay in social interaction or communication. In terms of quality, a professional may also look at the child's ability to sustain eye contact, social interaction and engage with others for a longer length of time. When a child moves from place to place in a preschool setting without showing an intent to reach out to others one may notice the quality of the interactions lacks consistency. Sometimes a child will do some things quickly, but his or her responses are so brief with a lack of full understanding or persistence that the response seems inadequate to sustain or fully engage with other people in social activities and social situations.

Questions to Consider

How can professionals better explain to parents that their child has a 'risk of autism' or is showing signs of autism?

What should a parent do if they think a preschool teacher may have misread a child's action or behavior in the preschool setting?

How can communication about autism be improved between parents and the schools?

What are some placement options in the school setting for children with autism and or developmental delays?

How can parents address the needs of their child if they feel he or she is in an ineffective educational program?

Additional Autism Exploration Topics

Autism School Placement Options

Creative Teaching Approaches in Autism Classrooms

Autism and Shared Experiences

Autism and the Impact of Making Transitions

Helping Children with Autism Address Fear

How Professionals Misinterpret Autism

Explaining Autism Eligibility

Autism Perspectives of Parents

Teaching Perspectives of Autism

Confusion about Disorders similar to Autism

RECOMMENDED READING FOR AUTISM

Peterson, S. (2013). *Is my child autistic or delayed?*

Is My Child Autistic or Delayed? is a book geared for parents and professionals to examine autism concerns and developmental delays in children. The book is parent friendly written in easy to understand language. It would also benefit college students learning to work with parents and early childhood students with delays and autism concerns. Parent concerns in many areas are presented from a school psychologist's perspective of the concern.

The book is also focused to help professionals as it gives an overview of different autism characteristics. *Is My Child Autistic or Delayed?* explores the multidisciplinary team approach in the decision making process of whether a child is delayed or has autism characteristics.

Is My Child Autistic or Delayed? is a wonderful resource for parents (and professionals) beginning the process of an educational assessment for possible autism concerns and developmental delays.

Is My Child Autistic or Delayed? is available in both print and ebook versions and was selected for the **Gold Winner in the 2014 eLit Awards**, a **Silver Winner in the 2013 Global Ebook Awards** program and the **2014 West Mountain Regional Reader Views Book** awards program.

Peterson, S, (2014). *Questionable Autism*

The book *Questionable Autism* is focused on opening discussions about a variety of autism topics from many viewpoints. Looking at professional, parenting, research and testing issues numerous questions are developed to consider the broad impact of autism topics for both parents and professionals across settings. Author Susan Louise Peterson weaves her experiences as an educator and school psychologist in the early childhood field into a discussion of some of the major issues impacting the field of autism. *Questionable Autism* includes many real world examples and experiences related to parenting topics, field issues and general practices in the area of autism. *Questionable Autism* has opened the door for broader discussions of many elements in the field autism.

INDEX

A
Ability, 24
Actions, 28,39,90
Activities, 3
Aloneness, 16
Assistance, 46
Associated conditions, 93
Attention, 29, 71,72
Attempts, 75
Attributes, 3
Atypicality, 19
Autism aspects, 63
Awareness of objects, 79

B
Behavior changes, 49
Boundaries, 35

C
Change, 36
Changes, 49
Closeness, 31
Cognitive ability, 32
Communication attempts, 75

Communication delay, 33
Conditions, 87
Connections, 43
Control, 9-10

D

Danger, 38
Delay, 33
Delayed engagement, 70
Delayed response, 58
Demands, 69
Details, 26
Differences, 37
Difficulties, 53
Directed generalization, 64
Disconnection, 77
Disengagement, 54
Distraction, 78

E

Eligibility, 84
Empathy, 18
Engagement, 53, 70
Expectations, 24
Experience, 48
Exploration, 6
Eye contact, 7

F
Fascination, 27
Fearful, 46
Features, 23
Flags, 86
Fleeting, 5
Flexibility, 12
Functional impact, 68

G
Generalization, 47, 64
Giftedness, 32
Greeting, 76

H
Habits, 26
Head banging, 35
Humor, 5

I
Impact, 68
Indicators, 83
Inflexibility, 67
Intensity, 11
Interaction, 56
Interest, 65
Interventions, 98

J
Joint attention, 72

K
Keyed up, 43

L
Language, 40
Lack of shared attention, 56

M
Meaningful play, 57
Misinterpretations, 95
Mismatch, 89
Misjudging signs, 91
Misread actions, 90

N
Need, 42

O
Objects, 71
Obsessive actions, 28
Oversensitivity, 30
Overlap, 94

P

Parenting skills, 44

Participation, 51

Perspectives, 88

Placement, 97

Play, 53

Preferred activities, 14

Prevent, 58

Program, 79

Q

Quality, 99

Questions, 20, 40, 60, 80, 100

R

Reciprocity, 66

Red flag, 92

Relationship, 52

Repetitive manner, 27

Resistance to change, 59

Response, 58

Request, 69

Risks, 87

Rote skills, 13

S

Sameness, 25
Self control, 10
Settings, 50
Selective relationships, 74
Service request, 45
Shared attention, 55
Skills, 44
Signs, 86
Situations, 3
Sleep issues, 35
Smile, 4
Social cues, 73
Social greeting, 76
Social smile, 4
Staring, 8
Symptoms, 85, 94

T

Tantrums, 34
Task, 52
Temporary behavior, 17
Time, 35
Tremor, 36

U

Unpredictable, 41

V

Variations, 96

Variety of settings, 46

W

Withdrawal, 17

AFTERWORD

Even though I worked as a school psychologist for years in a school district with many caring professionals (having years of training and experiences) there were always some differences in how each professional viewed the condition of a child. One professional would see a certain characteristic stand out in a child, while another professional may notice something else. Some professionals had nursing or health related backgrounds and they would suggest medical conditions that seemed to describe a child while other professionals were more behavior focused when they looked at a child. Some professionals were family focused and quickly noticed sibling relationships, family structure and dynamics that influenced a child's actions and behaviors. Educational professionals would sometimes focus an assessment on figuring out strategies to help the child in the classroom setting. Those with a social work background were helpful in finding resources to improve the child and family situation. The book, **Possible Autism** has focused on taking a second look at some of the signs and symptoms of autism and seeing that a simple parent issue can be looked at with many possibilities that could describe a child in a number of ways. Understanding a child's autism eligibility is not a perfect process so looking at other possibilities can help in developing a more complete picture of the child in an educational setting.

www.ingramcontent.com/pod-product-compliance
Lightning Source LLC
Chambersburg PA
CBHW031424290426
44110CB00011B/508